"HERNDON IS SAYING 'PAY ATTENTION'

But he means pay attention the way a novelist or a poet pays attention—see, hear, feel the life throbbing through these youngsters as they build their monster kites, horse around, take photomat pictures of their private parts, and alternately hassle and comfort one another."
—Life

"A beautiful book, beautiful . . . Herndon's special, very special, genius is his novelist's feel for the gift of eccentricity, for the perishable quality of every child's singularity. He tells stories about children—especially about Piston and Richard—that break my heart . . . Men like him may save us yet."
—Geoffrey Wolff, Newsweek

"I didn't think that anyone, not even James Herndon, could write a book better, funnier, truer and more to the point than his The Way It Spozed to Be. But he has."
—John Holt, author of How Children Fail

"Like Vonnegut, Herndon writes a very enjoyable, seemingly off-the-cuff kind of book that keeps you thinking over bits and pieces long after you've read it . . . What Herndon has vividly conveyed is the great, occasional and accidental joy which would be our only reward."
—The New York Times

"Huckleberry Finn, updated to the 1960's."
—San Francisco Chronicle

Bantam Books by James Herndon

HOW TO SURVIVE IN YOUR NATIVE LAND
THE WAY IT SPOZED TO BE

HOW
TO SURVIVE
IN YOUR
NATIVE LAND

James Herndon

A NATIONAL GENERAL COMPANY

RLI: $\dfrac{\text{VLM 7 (VLR 6-7)}}{\text{IL 10-up}}$

HOW TO SURVIVE IN YOUR NATIVE LAND
*A Bantam Book / published by arrangement with
Simon & Schuster, Inc.*

PRINTING HISTORY
Simon & Schuster edition published 1971
Bantam edition published April 1972
2nd printing

*Bantam Books are published by Bantam Books, Inc., a National
General company. Its trade-mark, consisting of the words "Bantam
Books" and the portrayal of a bantam, is registered in the United
States Patent Office and in other countries. Marca Registrada.
Bantam Books, Inc., 666 Fifth Avenue, New York, N.Y. 10019.*

PRINTED IN THE UNITED STATES OF AMERICA

FOR JAY AND JACK

Contents

PART ONE

PART TWO • EXPLANATORY NOTES

vii

PART THREE

James Thurber once sat by his window watching men cut down elm trees to clear a site for an institution in which to confine people who had been driven insane by the cutting down of elm trees.

HOW TO SURVIVE IN
YOUR NATIVE LAND

Part One

Work, knowledge and love, Reich said, are the well-springs of human life. Who could argue with that?

—FROM LEFT,
by *Keith Jones*

Chapter I

A Kite

I might as well begin with Piston. Piston was, as
a matter of description, a red-headed medium-
sized chubby eighth grader; his definitive characteristic
was, however, stubbornness. Without going into a lot of
detail, it became clear right away that what Piston didn't
want to do, Piston didn't do; what Piston did want to do,
Piston did.

It really wasn't much of a problem. Piston wanted
mainly to paint, draw monsters, scratch designs on mimeograph blanks and print them up, write an occasional horror story—some kids referred to him as The Ghoul—and
when he didn't want to do any of those, he wanted to
roam the halls and on occasion (we heard) investigate
the girls' bathrooms.

We had minor confrontations. Once I wanted everyone
to sit down and listen to what I had to say—something
about the way they had been acting in the halls. I was
letting them come and go freely and it was up to them
(I planned to point out) not to raise hell so that I had to
hear about it from other teachers. Sitting down was the
issue—I was determined everyone was going to do it first,
then I'd talk. Piston remained standing. I re-ordered. He
paid no attention. I pointed out that I was talking to
him. He indicated he heard me. I inquired then why in
hell didn't he sit down. He said he didn't want to. I said

I did want him to. He said that didn't matter to him. I said do it anyway. He said why? I said because I said so. He said he wouldn't. I said Look I want you to sit down and listen to what I'm going to say. He said he *was* listening. I'll listen but I won't sit down.

Well, that's the way it goes sometimes in schools. You as teacher become obsessed with an issue—I was the injured party, conferring, as usual, unheard-of freedoms, and here they were as usual taking advantage. It ain't pleasant coming in the teachers' room for coffee and having to hear somebody say that so-and-so and so-and-so from *your* class were out in the halls *without a pass* and *making faces* and *giving the finger* to kids in *my* class during the most *important* part of *my* lesson about *Egypt* —and you ought to be allowed your tendentious speech, and most everyone will allow it, sit down for it, but occasionally someone wises you up by refusing to submit where it isn't necessary. But anyway, it's not the present point, which is really only Piston's stubbornness. Another kid told me that when Piston's father got mad at him and punished him, as Piston thought, unjustly (one cannot imagine Piston considering any punishment just), Piston got up in the middle of the night, went into the garage and revenged himself on his father's car. Once he took out and threw away two spark plugs. Another time he managed to remove all the door handles. You get a nice picture of Piston sitting quiet all evening long brooding about not being allowed to watch some favorite science-fiction program because he'd brought home a note about unsatisfactory this-or-that at school, sitting there unresponding and impassive, and then his father getting up in the morning to go to work, perhaps in a hurry or not feeling well, trying to start the car or looking at the locked doors and rolled up windows and the places where the door handles had been pried off. How did any of us get into this? we ought to be asking ourselves.

It was probably Frank Ramirez who brought up the idea of making kites. Frank was a teacher, not a kid;

4

we were working together. All the kids were making them suddenly; they scrounged the schoolrooms and maddened the shop teachers looking for suitable lengths of wood. Frank brought in fancy paper. The kites were wonderful. Naturally we plunged down to the lower field to fly them. They flew well, or badly, or not at all, crashed and were broken, sailed away, got caught in overhead wires, the kids ran and yelled and cried and accused one another. It went on for several days and of course we heard a lot about classes overlooking the lower field being interrupted in the most important parts of the lessons about Egypt, for after all those kids wanted to know why they couldn't be flying kites instead of having Egypt, and Frank and I were cocky enough to state aloud that indeed we also wondered why they couldn't be flying kites too, after all who was stopping them? Piston, up in Room 45, was preparing our comeuppance.

Piston had been making a kite for several days. He continued making it while others were flying theirs. It had only one definitive characteristic too; it was huge. The cross-pieces were 1 × 2 boards. The covering was heavy butcher paper, made heavier by three coats of poster paint in monstrous designs. The cord was clothes-line rope. It was twenty feet long. Piston was finished with his kite about the time when everyone else had finished with the whole business of making and flying kites and had settled down in the room anticipating a couple of weeks of doing nothing, resting up for some future adventure. Piston produced his finished product, which was universally acclaimed a masterpiece. It was. Pictorially monstrous as usual, its *size,* its heavy *boards,* its *rope,* aroused a certain amount of real awe. Piston was really something else, we could see that. None of us had had such a concept.

But when Piston announced he was prepared to fly it, we all hooted, relieved. It was easier to have Piston-the-nut back again than to put up with Piston-the-genius-artist. No one had thought of it as something to fly—only as something to look at and admire. In any case, it clearly

5

would not fly. It was too big, too heavy, too awkward, unbalanced, there wasn't enough wind, you couldn't run with it—we had lots of reasons. Stubborn Piston hauled it down to the field past amazed windows of classbound kids ignoring Egypt once again to goggle and exclaim. Down on the grass we all gathered around the inert monster. If nothing else, Frank and I thought, Piston had prepared a real scene, something memorable—David being drawn through the streets of Florence.

The kite flew. Piston had prepared no great scene. Instead he had (I think) commanded the monster kite to fly. So it flew. Of course it flew. Two of the biggest and strongest boys were persuaded to run with the kite; Piston ran with the rope. Everyone participated in what was believed to be a charade. We would act as if we thought the kite would fly. It would be in itself a gas. They ran; he pulled. The kite lumbered into the air, where it stayed aloft menacingly for perhaps four or five minutes. Then it dove, or rather just fell like a stone (like an avalanche!), with a crash. When it crashed, everyone was seized with a madness and rushed to the kite, jumped on it, stomped it, tore it . . . all except Frank and I, and we wanted to. (Great difficulties at that very moment were angrily reported to us later by teachers of Egypt classes.)

The kite was saved, though. Piston repaired and repapered it, repainted it. Frank and I hung it in the room and admired it, and forgot it. But next week, Lou, the principal, approached us at lunchtime with great excitement. What about Piston? he wanted to know, and what about that Kite? Whose idea . . . ? and so on. His concern was not Egypt, but the fact that Piston and others had taken it out to the playground during lunch and flown it again. So? So! screamed Lou, the goddamn thing was a menace! It weighed a hundred pounds. It fell down and damn near killed thirty or forty seventh grade girls, and their mothers were calling him up and was this Piston crazy or were we, or what? And he wanted it made clear that flying that kite was out! O-U-T, out! He had enough troubles with our goddamn class running around

6

all over the place and other teachers griping and smoking in the bathrooms and parents complaining they weren't learning nothing and he'd always supported us but he couldn't have that giant kite. Couldn't have it! We soothed him, agreeing to tell Piston in no uncertain terms and so on. We walked outside with Lou, who had calmed down and had begun admiring the kite in retrospect, realizing that there was no way such a creation could fly (*aerodynamically speaking,* he said), and yet it did fly and this Piston or whatever his name was must be a pretty exceptional kid, and we were agreeing and realizing what a great guy Lou was for a principal even if, we reminded him, he had goofed up our schedule for this marvelous class we'd planned which had resulted in that extraordinary kite and other grand exploits, along with, we admitted, a certain amount of difficulty for him, Lou, and how well he'd handled it and supported us and . . . when Lou suddenly screamed Aaarrghhh! and fell back. I thought he'd been stung by a bee—we'd had a lot of bees that year, which also interrupted Egypt quite a bit, flying in the classroom where kids could scream with fake or real fear or try to kill them by throwing objects, often Egypt books, at them, exempt from retribution by the claim that they were just trying to save some *allergic kid* from *death*—but then he screamed There it is again! and pointed up, and there was The Monster From Outer Space, seventy-five feet up, plunging and wheeling and lurching through the thin air, a ton of boards and heavy paper and ghouls and toothy vampires leering down at an amazed lunchtime populace of little seventh grade girls, all with mothers and phones. Jesus Christ, look out! yelled Lou, and rushed for the playground, just as the giant came hurtling down like a dead flying mountain. It crashed; seventh grade girls scattered. (Their mothers reached for the phones.) Kids rushed from every direction and hurled themselves at the kite. They stomped it and tore it and killed it in wildest glee. They lynched it and murdered it and executed it and mercy-killed it and put it out of its misery, and when it was over and Lou had everyone pulled off the scattered corpse of the kite and sitting down on benches and shut up there was nothing left of it but bits and pieces of painted butcher paper and 1×2 boards and clothesline rope.

Chapter II

Son of }
Return of } Way It Spozed to Be

About a third of the way through Kurt Vonnegut's novel *Slaughterhouse Five*, the hero became "unstuck in time" and saw a World War II movie backwards. Seen thus, every hurtful blow of war was turned into a healing act. The bombers, which took off backwards from English fields, were full of holes and wounded men. The German fighter planes they met "sucked bullets and shell fragments from some of the planes and crewmen. They did the same for wrecked American bombers on the ground and those planes flew up backwards to join the formation."

Over a German city in flames, the bombers sucked up the bombs from the ground and made the flames go out by a "miraculous magnetism." They stored the bombs in racks inside the planes and flew them backwards to England, where the bombs were unloaded and sent by rail to factories. There women took the bombs apart and turned them back into minerals. "The minerals were then shipped to specialists in remote areas. It was their business to put them into the ground, to hide them cleverly, so they would never hurt anybody ever again."

That movie, unstuck in time, showed him a world unaccountably in holocaust, showed him the familiar apparatus of war now employed to cure and heal men and cities. I suppose it to be the absolutely perfect image for us now in America. For so many of us now see America as all wrong. If we are forty or so, we may see it—considering we were around during that same World War II —as *unaccountably* all wrong. And we hope to use the familiar apparatus of America—not only those fires, those bombs, but the whole institutional structure of America— as an agent to heal and cure, to transform by "miraculous magnetism" bad into good, horror into beauty. We dream that it will again become an agent of fruitfulness—the power which will tell us the right questions to ask in order to restore the wasted land, cause the stagnant streams to flow and fish to leap, heal The Maimed King and form, as King Arthur said, a more perfect union. We hope to become unstuck in time.

I am also addicted to another more common image, that of the road or voyage. The best expression of it is in Ortega—that man has no nature excepting the road he has traveled. So that in *The Way It Spozed To Be* I wrote a travelogue. The people who read the book and wrote me about it seemed either to recognize that land as one in which they too traveled or lived, or as one so uncharted and astonishing that they had difficulty believing in it. Only Mr. Friedenberg wanted to point out that *The Way It Spozed To Be* was an "account of the author's own gradual growth and commitment" and that it was just that commitment which put him at odds with things along that road. And that is exactly our situation, or The Problem, as they say, in America. We hope to find our work, our growth and our commitment within the institutions of our country, and in fact that is where, to some degree, we do find them—only to discover that as we do so we are more and more extruded, or if we are not, we grow to distrust ourselves.

In 1957, having spent six years in Europe, living here and there, doing this and that, I was working in a small-time military-industrial-complex-American-government agency operating in an abandoned pants factory

10

on the outskirts of Paris. Fran and I had married and were expecting our first child. We decided to go back to America.

I was perhaps happier about it than Fran. But then, I had invented an ideology for going back. Briefly, I had the idea that America needed me. The mainstream of America needed me, Jim Herndon, traveler, *voyageur,* precisely because I had traveled a different road. Certainly I would be welcome as a teacher, for instance, if only as an antidote to the kinds of teachers I had known as a child. Of course, it was possible I was misled by reading French newspapers. Who colonized the West if not those same *voyageurs?*

But it wasn't just one-way. If America needed me, I needed it in order to get serious. Besides, another good reason for going back was that I suspected we were both about to get fired and if that happened, we'd lost that free transportation back to America. We were anxious to collect it. What we were about to get fired for was the sin of not being able to get serious about our jobs. Fran especially couldn't be serious about not leaving them classified documents laying out overnight in plain sight of spies, Frogs and suspicious cats of all sorts. I couldn't get serious about revising files full of indignant letters from French contractors and complaints about airfields sinking into the mud of sourthern France.

Back in America, we sat in our New York hotel bar, drinking gin and tonics in the summertime, watching three ball games at once on the TV, waiting around for our government-paid plane tickets to San Francisco, via North Carolina. I'd never seen any TV at all, let alone a ball game, and here, all at once, the Yankees were playing Cleveland, the New York Giants were playing the Milwaukee Braves, the Brooklyn Dodgers were playing somebody. Long time ago when I left America, I'd spent two days in New York, and on both days the Yankees were playing Cleveland and I went to those games in Yankee Stadium. You have to realize what all this means to someone who spent his youth lying on the sofa on sultry L.A.

11

afternoons listening to the radio purring out play-by-play accounts of ball games from Chicago, St. Louis, New York . . . Johnny Mize hit winning homers in the ninth of both those games, the evil bastard, one of them off Mike Garcia, my idol. Luke Easter, my other idol, pulled a groin muscle in the first game—that was all he did.

When, a year after we returned, the Giants moved to San Francisco, where we lived, I felt vindicated. Mainstream America was moving in my direction. The Giants were playing in Seal Stadium. We could go. We could sit in the bleachers for ninety cents and make bets. We could watch Willie Mays, if not Monte Irvin. I'd had a job in the mountains. Jay was two years old. I'd had a job in Oakland. We had an apartment in North Beach, where the poets were writing poetry and reading it aloud and we could hear it and mainstream America was flowing uphill. I knew that I was part of it, playing the right side of the street. I was getting serious. I had been fired. I had a job in Tierra Firma on the outskirts of town. I had work to do. I was playing ball, in America, within that apparatus.

It is hard for me to imagine now why I had such notions, but I know that I did. Perhaps my idea of mainstream America has changed. I had the idea that one could find work to do and that being able to work was what was needed. Well, we have disagreed, America and I, about the nature of the work one ought to do, yet on the whole I think I was right back then. You must find work to do in your country and you can find it, or you could ten years ago.

In *The Way It Spozed To Be* I was able to write that the book was about my "teaching, learning to teach" in a public school in America. As a travelogue it was mercifully cut short—the end of the novice traveler's voyage brought about simply, perhaps by lack of funds or by losing his passport out the window of an Italian train. Returning, the traveler may describe the high points of his trip, the pleasures, the difficulties, *what it was like* and remark his determination to re-embark. He wants to do it

12

over again, do it right this time. Perhaps he wants to stay ten years.

This book is about what it is like to work from 1959 to 1969 in America. A decade, comrades. Of course it is about schools, too, since that is where I have worked along this way. I got rather sarcastic with myself when I began to write this. What? Another school book? I'll call it *Return of Way It Spozed To Be!* I told myself; I'll call it *Son of Way It Spozed To Be!* Yet one purpose of writing, like the purpose of talking to other people, is to demonstrate to yourself that you aren't crazy. Once begun, good or bad, such a purpose becomes immune to sarcasm. So I end up with only this chapter entitled both.

I've started off about two or three years after I began to work in schools again. That is about the time when you begin to feel that you know what you are doing, when you've gotten good recommendations for doing what you are supposed to do a couple of years, and that means you are going to have a job and get paid and be able to go to work and you know you need to have those things —and so you come to work one year ready to make changes. You are confident and you know what to do and you can do it and you are going to—all of a sudden you realize that's what you have in mind—you are going to change that fucking system by demonstrating to it how to work, how to teach, what education is, really. You are going to change it by using that system itself, you are going to use those fires, bombs, machine guns, institutions, B-52's, you are going to change them instruments of death and repression and ignorance into instruments of work, knowledge and love.

So that is what I planned to write about, and I will as best I can. But in fact the book is mostly about kites and dogs and lizards and salamanders and magic and what people I know or got to know did, on occasion, during that decade. Those things are what remain clear and they are what I know really happened and the rest is very hazy. Not only that, but the details—those dogs and so on—turn out to be the reasons for your work, and thus the very fundaments of whatever knowledge and love you get. Bonuses—unaccountable rewards. If you only work in order to change things, you will simply go nuts. I am an authority on it.

So, *Do Whatever You Think Is Right,* as Owen says in the novel *Left*—but in the meantime (I would add) keep an eye out for bees flying in the classroom, and for edible plants along the road.

Chapter III

Christopher Columbus

Thus: about a month before the end of one
school year, Frank Ramirez and I invented a
course for the next year. We thought up a simple notion.
We wanted a two-hour class, and we wanted to both be
there at the same time. We wanted the class to be free of
certain restrictions—those regarding curriculum, those regarding grades and those regarding school behavior rules,
mainly the ones about leaving the classroom.

We didn't think there ought to be any difficulties in
arranging it, and at the same time we prepared to answer
all the difficulties logically. The two-hour class was O.K.
because the eighth grade kids had two electives anyway;
they could just choose to take our class instead of two
others. We would arrange to have the class the last two
periods in the day (seventh and eighth); since all teachers
got a preparation period (a free period, but you weren't
supposed to call it *free*), we'd take ours seventh and
eighth respectively and spend our *free* time teaching together in the classroom in our new class. We were making,
we planned to point out, a sacrifice. The kids would enroll
voluntarily and we'd notify parents about what kind of
course it was. We sent out notices and held a meeting
of kids who thought they might want to enroll.

Everything worked out fine. There was no trouble. We
were perhaps a bit disappointed. The principal agreed.

15

The vice-principal agreed. The counselors agreed. Perhaps the parents agreed; they abstained at least, since none sent back comment. There were really only two difficulties. First, the schedule didn't work out. When we got back to school in the fall, we found out that Lou had forgotten to schedule our prep periods right, so that we couldn't work the class in the same room at the same time for two hours. Lou merely said he was sorry he forgot it, and declined to make any changes then, at the beginning of school. He couldn't see why we were pissed off; he considered it a minor matter. We felt the whole course had been sabotaged.

The other difficulty was with the kids. About twenty-five kids showed up, clearly divided in their intentions. A few were really looking forward to having two periods of time to do stuff in—our emphasis had been on the arts, generally, and they planned to paint and write and put on plays. The rest had only been attracted by the *no assignment* and *no grade* promise in our presentation; they came in wising off and horsing around, equally clearly prepared to disbelieve and test us out. As for that great rest of the school kid population who weren't in fact there, it's clear they just considered the whole thing a trap or a shuck. They knew they could put up with the ordinary school routine, having done it seven years already, but who knew what might happen to them if they risked something new?

Besides the intentions of the kids, of course, there was also the fact of our intention—Frank's and mine. I think that is best expressed by this: we would do, as the main thing, all the stuff we did in our regular classes as a sideline when the regular "work" was finished.

Frank had been working at the school for perhaps eight or nine years. In the two or three years I'd been there, I learned from watching him how to conduct yourself as a regular teacher in regular classes in a regular school. How you could teach and work there without driving yourself nuts with boredom, rage, a sense of your own hypocrisy,

16

without unending uproars with the administration and parents and without getting fired, which was important to me. Frank was the best at this I ever saw. He filled his room with art materials, even though he was supposed to be teaching English and social studies to seventh graders. While other teachers were complaining publicly how difficult it was in the short time of nine months to "get through" the "material" in the texts, Frank announced that the stuff you were supposed to teach in a year could be handled easily in six weeks or so, and you had the rest of the time to do other things you might care to do. He figured the other teachers dragged out the teaching of Egypt or math all year because they didn't have anything else they wanted to do or cared about, or because they were afraid of the kids once the threat of the curriculum was called off.

In Language Arts, he showed the kids how to diagram sentences, pointed out the parts of speech, showed them where to put commas and semicolons—all in quite a short time. He was the only man I've ever heard give a good answer to that old kid question, Why do we have to make these diagrams?

Why? Because they are beautiful, said Frank. What Frank understood, or knew how to work, or knew how to involve the kids in, or something . . . was a kind of interrelationship between studies, which were supposed to be real, and fantasy, which was supposed to be not-real. So that if they were "studying" some place which was an island, they studied it O.K., read the book, answered them questions on ditto sheets, and then the kids would find themselves with big pieces of paper inventing an island, drawing and painting in its geography, describing its people, its kings and rulers, the way the people ate, or what they lived in, or how they celebrated Christmas. Or they went to the library and got books and wrote to the authors, and put the authors' answers up on the board, telling where they were born and how they got the idea of writing such and such a kid's book. Then Frank might give some letters to other kids, who would write secret answers as if they were the authors and these would go up on the board too. He took kids to the Golden Gate Bridge, where they dropped off bottles with fake notes in them into the outgoing tide and the answers to these notes, from points up and down the California coast, went up on the board too, along with "environments" made from junk in cigar boxes and illustrations from books or stories which he made the kids paint left-handed with big brushes on small pieces of paper so their technique or lack of it wouldn't get in the way.

I joined him in this kind of work. In my class we wrote to the Peace Corps and got real information about the problems of various countries and the straight dope on what the Corps hoped to do in these countries, how they would work, and so on. The kids, pretending to be Peace Corps workers themselves, wrote imaginary journals of stays in Africa and South America; the idea was that they would use the official information in their writing and would solve a lot of problems. In fact, though, their journals were full of first-class air travels to and from the countries, drinking cocktails and making it with stewardesses or *white hunters* in the *bush,* torture by *natives,* escapes, liaisons with chiefs' daughters, buried treasures and elephants' graveyards. Little attention was given to the raising of chickens, the building of irrigation systems, or the growing of flax. Medical care was brought in only as accessory to a needed miracle—the chief's son cured by a shot of penicillin just when the Corpsman was about to be eaten up by head-hunting pygmies.

In English, I had the kids begin inventing languages. They wrote down lists of common words and when we had the lists we'd start making a picture or symbol to stand for it, just like them Egyptians did. Then we'd choose the best symbol and make lists of those and after we had a couple of hundred or so we'd start translating simple fairy tales into our new language, or making up stories to write in it, and put the stories on huge decorated pieces of paper and send them over to Frank's class to see if they could decipher them, as if they were Linear B.

Sooner or later there would be an item in the school newspaper about it:

The kids in Rooms 45 and 31 are making up their own languages in their class. Here is an example of it; can you figure it out?

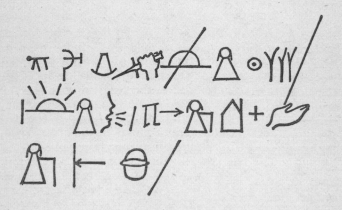

A couple of teachers would say That sounds like an interesting project and point out its relationship to Egypt to me. But, like the fake Peace Corps, where other teachers were always faintly disappointed when these journals, put on display in the library, failed to follow the government plans (the kids weren't using the information from official sources, and so it followed that they weren't learning anything, and so it wasn't social studies, but only fantasy)—the article failed to display the real point of such an activity. It failed to show the tremendous uproar when twenty kids rushed to the board to put up their symbols, the arguments of kids about which was best, and the fine look of the decorated pages when they were done.

It also failed to show my pleasure at symbols which I thought just right, like these:

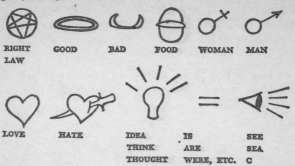

My pleasure was also in the process of the symbols working out. *Right* started out as a complicated drawing of a sheriff, *good* as an angel, *bad* as the devil—then they were refined into the star, halo and horns. We talked about the necessity of briefer, less complicated forms, since we wouldn't want to do all the drawing every time we Egyptians sent a note to a friend. Later on we learned from ourselves, and the symbols became simpler right away, as in *think* and *is*. We went on and made certain kinds of words different colors when we made posters, blue for things, red for actions, green for descriptions and so on, following the familiar pattern of seventh grade pedants. I pushed it a bit further, trying to make the changeover from ideograph to alphabet, so that a symbol which once meant only *good* came to represent *G* while retaining the meaning of good.

We went on and on with it. Too much! I thought to myself all the time, full of excitement and pride, it is a great lesson. We are inventing, we are learning parts of speech and puns and structure of language and intricacies of grammar—all participating, with fun, uproar, excitement, consultant approval, letters from the superintendent saying as how Frank and I were creative teachers, A's for the kids, Frank and I coming to work feeling good and ready to go, happy parents—and we all lived through a kind of Golden Age of Rooms 31 and 45 at Spanish Main School. I mean we were a big success—more importantly *I* was; Frank had already been one for some time.

In this marvelous confident mood we approached the beginning of the year in Creative Arts. We had more ideas than you could shake a stick at.

For most of that year Frank and I agreed that CA—as the school soon began calling it—was absolutely the worst class we could have imagined. Nothing worked right. We had a lot to blame it on, griping to each other, commiserating together, telling each other it wasn't our fault. It was the administration's fault for one thing, scheduling things wrong. Then it was the kids' fault, for not being the right kind of kids. It was also the school's fault, for manifesting an atmosphere in which you wouldn't do anything unless you were made to.

In fact, another two main things—of a quite different nature, and yet quite firmly connected—were at fault. The first was what had seemed to us a detail and concerned leaving class. On the very first day we issued Permanent Hall Passes, each with a particular kid's name on it, and told the kids they could come and go in and out of our classrooms at any time, without asking permission or leave, and they could go anywhere around the school grounds. If stopped they had only to show their passes. We announced this casually; it seemed simple and obvious to us. One of the biggest drags in a school is the fact that whenever a kid wants to go anywhere, or whenever you want to send a kid somewhere to get something or do something, you have to stop and write out a pass, sign it, date it, put down the time and his expected destination. If you didn't, then the kid was sure to get stopped by some adult in the halls or wherever he was and get in trouble for being in the halls without a pass. Then the kid would come back to you, sometimes with the adult in question or with some goofy Rally Boy or Rally Girl who was On Duty at the time, and demand that you save him from detention or calling his mom for this sin, and you'd have to say Yeah, I sent him out, or Yeah, I said he could go . . . then like as not the kid hadn't gone where you said for him to go or where he said he was going, and so you had to go into that, and in the end everyone was mad and nothing had been accomplished, except maybe the kid had gotten his smoke in the bathroom, supposing that was what he wanted.

Being smart, we got around all that with the Permanent Hall Passes. The kids were ecstatic, and spent quite a bit of time that first day interrogating us as to what we really meant. They kept it up so long I finally got mad and yelled that it meant they could leave anytime, go anywhere on the grounds, that yes, once and for all yes, that was what it meant and if anyone said another word about it I was pulling back these passes and it was all off. Then they believed it.

The second thing was that all the great notions we had, all the ideas for things to do, all our apparatus for insuring a creative, industrious, happy, meaningful class didn't seem to excite the kids all that much. Most of the kids didn't want to do any of them at all, anytime. They didn't want to write to the Peace Corps, they didn't want to bring cigar boxes and make avant-garde environments, they didn't want to make plaster statuary, they didn't want to write stories, they didn't want to paint left-handed or make up new languages . . . they didn't want to do a fucking thing except use that fucking Permanent Hall Pass in the way it was supposed to be used, namely to take it and leave the class, roam around, come back in, leave again, roam around and come back in. When they went out they would say *There's Nothing To Do Around Here,* and leave, and when they came back they would say *There's Nothing To Do Out There,* and everyone would agree and say that awhile and bitch about the number of adults and narc Rally Boys who made them show their pass and brag to each other about how they told off the chickenshit narcs of all sorts . . . and for the first few days we were besieged by teachers and Rally Boys asking were those unbelievable *Permanent Hall Passes* valid and we'd say yes, and then for a few more days we were visited by kids who had invented excuses to get out of class in order to drop by and ask us urgently if it were really true that we had given out *Permanent Hall Passes* to *Every Kid* in our *Class,* and we'd say Yes! . . . and after those gripes and narratives had run out of interest someone would remember to say There's Nothing To Do In Here again, and out most of the kids would go.

Well, as a lesson plan, there is nothing I can recommend quite so highly as a Permanent Hall Pass. After a while, Frank and I, on the edge of complete despair, began to figure out what was wrong with the ideas that had worked so well in our regular classes. It was very simple. Why did the kids in regular class like to do all that inventive stuff? Why, only because it was better than the regular stuff. If you wrote a fake journal pretending to be Tutankhamen's favorite embalmer, it was better than reading the dull Text, answering Questions on ditto sheets, Discussing, making Reports, or taking Tests. Sure it was better—not only that but you knew the teacher liked it better for some insane reason which you didn't have to understand and you would get better grades for it than you were used to getting in social studies or English. But that only applied to a regular class where it was clear you had to (1) stay there all period and (2) you had to be doing something or you might get an F. Take away those two items, as Frank and I had done in all innocence, and you get a brief vision of the truth.

We were in a new world. Nothing can be worse than that. We had to face the fact that all the stuff we thought the kids were dying to do (if they only had time away from the stupefying lessons of other teachers) was in fact stuff that *we* wanted them to do, that *we* invented, that interested *us*—not only that but it interested us mainly as things to be doing during periods of time when something had to be going on, when no one was supposed to be just sitting around doing nothing. And not only things to be doing—it was things for *them,* the kids, to be doing.

Things we wanted to see them do, the results of which we wanted to see. We wanted to see what symbols the kids would invent for English words; we didn't have much curiosity about the symbols we ourselves would invent. We didn't write fake Peace Corps journals ourselves; we only told the kids to do it. I don't mean to criticize us harshly on these points; that is, by and large, the attitude of teachers and it's a normal rationale for teaching. You want to see what the kids can do, you want to get some idea of their abilities, their intelligence, their cleverness, their ingenuity, their—creativity. You want to have something interesting to do during the class time. It was clear that many kids rather liked the writing or the painting or constructing or whatever it was, once they got started (since they had to do something) and once it was finished, once the other kids expressed admiration, once they got an A, once their work was shown in the room on Back to School Night. Looked at that way, we were able to decide that we had a lot more ideas than the kids and the kids never knew what they wanted to do anyway, and if we made them do stuff we knew was interesting and exciting and all, they would be better off for it. About the sixth week of CA, we laid that out to the kids and tried to establish a hard line.

Since no one is doing anything, *then therefore,* we told them, sat down in their seats and quiet, you'll have to do assignments. We told them how great the assignments would be. That was going to be that.

Indignation, disappointment and sneers greeted my own pronouncement. I was told in plain words that I was being chickenshit. I was reminded of my brave words *when I talked them into taking this lousy course last year* (I'd thought no one was listening) and quite clearly informed that it was the same old thing—teachers promising "class participation in decision making" and then if it didn't work out just like the teacher wanted, the teacher then unilaterally changed his fucking mind. (I remind myself how things change when you give up your authority, officially, even if you really want to keep it, privately.

24

The kids begin to talk to you just as if you are a real person, and often say just what they mean.) I was informed that the only virtue of the class was its freedom to do (to come and go) and not-do; take away that and they all planned to see their counselors and ask for transfers.

I think I would have weathered that storm, stuck to the new hard line if it hadn't been for Meg, Lily, and Jane. Meg, Lily, and Jane were our heroes. They were doing just exactly what Frank and I had figured everyone would be doing in CA, namely, they were doing stuff all the time. The first day or so, one of the things the kids had in mind was to make a newspaper, a kids' newspaper (underground papers not having been invented yet) as opposed to the boring, tendentious adult-oriented official school paper which was mostly written by the teacher in charge anyway. Having decided that, most of the kids then made use of their passes to come and go and talk about nothing to do; Meg and Lily started off immediately to make the newspaper. Meg would get the material and edit it, Lily would type and run it off and figure how to distribute it, and Jane would do the illustrations. In the end, receiving absolutely no cooperation from anyone else, they had done it all themselves; Meg not only edited but wrote all the stories (no one else could stop coming in and out long enough to do so) and Lily talked the office into letting her use the mimeograph machine which was unheard of and Jane drew all sorts of stuff for it. Since that time, they had begun plans for a literary magazine to be called *Infinity,* and spent their time trying to persuade the other members of the class to write something for it. Having no luck whatsoever, they complained bitterly during that first six weeks about the other kids, how they wouldn't do anything, and how it was supposed to be a class project, and Frank and I would try to talk to the kids about writing, and about class solidarity and so on, but no use.

The point is, I had counted on support from these three in our new, reactionary notion of class. Surely they would be in favor of making the other kids write and paint and draw and so on, thus supplying them with material—but in fact, they weren't. They too threatened rebellion. Jane announced she would draw or paint nothing else that year if required to. Meg agreed that it was too bad that no one else wanted to write for the magazine, but that it was obvious that "enforced writing" (she said) wasn't going to be any good. She might as well be taking *Journalism,* she said, with noticeable disgust.

I tried arguments. How about the fact that they wanted to work and couldn't get anything done because everyone else was just screwing around? Wouldn't it be better if everyone wrote and drew for the magazine? Yes, they said, but only if they really wanted to. We went thus round and round. Meg, most brilliant and articulate of girls, told me that even in the regular journalism class there were only two or three people who really wanted to write for the paper and had any talent for it; the rest of the students, being forced to do so in order not to flunk, wrote only boring and rather stupid stuff. That, she said, was probably what caused the journalism teacher to have to rewrite most of the dull, boring stuff, and what made the whole paper thus sound like it had been written by a teacher, and after all, dull, boring stuff rewritten was still dull, boring stuff. Not only that, she said, isn't it so that good magazines are really put out by these very people who have talent and the desire to put them out? And isn't it so that most people in the world do not write, don't put out magazines, maybe don't even read them? But the magazines are good, sometimes, which was the point. Why should it be different in a class?

The fact that a magazine was good was the point. The desire of the teacher that everyone "participate" was beside the point and would surely result in a bad magazine. You couldn't have both, she was trying to tell me, and so you had to decide which you wanted.

Well, Frank and I decided without no trouble. Reaction would have to wait. Perhaps we only wanted to be reassured. The hall passes remained, and *Infinity* came out regularly. The class remained in a state of chaos, measured by ordinary school standards. Yet if I select *Infinity* as a measure (I think now), the class takes on a surprising aspect of solidarity. When an issue was ready to be put together, for instance, everyone knew it. They came that day prepared to collate the pages, staple them, serve as runners to bring twenty copies or so to every classroom (using Permanent Hall Passes to do so) and when all that was over they sat down to look at and read and comment on *Infinity* and criticize it and decide if this new issue was as good or better or worse than some previous issue just as if they were really involved in it. After the first issue, in any case, Meg didn't have to write at all and Jane didn't have to do all the drawings and Lily had more offers to help with the mimeograph machine than she could handle. The offers came from other kids in other classes. They did exist. Stories poured in. There were secret writers all over the place. Kids in CA read them and judged them. *Infinity* kept coming out. The whole class took credit for it, time and time again, and they were right. *We* are doing it, they said. After all, who else was?

Well. It was the class of Piston and the kite. I think that has already told most everything else. Frank and I continued to run between joy and desperation, constantly hassled because Egypt teachers complained to us about the Permanent Hall Pass kids giving their kids the finger seventh and eighth period as they passed by, because the secretaries were complaining that the kids were using too many mimeograph blanks and cluttering up the office and arguing with them about which should have priority, page fourteen of *Infinity* or some announcement from the administration about PTA meetings, continually anxious because it always looked like no one was doing anything, and because, for example, a marvelously bright girl like Marcia should have decided to use all her free gift of time in CA doing nothing all year except going around to the boys asking them stuff like *Have you seen*

Mike Hunt? (a nonexistent person whose name, translated into quick speech, turns out to be My Cunt)—a question which I'd heard asked myself a time or two when I was in the eighth grade and which had interested me then more than anything else in the entire whole wide world. We were bothered and confused and upset because the kids who never would do anything we suggested they might do were always the very kids who kept complaining to us that they were bored, that there was Nothing To Do In Here (and Out There), that We Never Do Anything In This Class and We Don't Learn Anything In Here. When we heard that complaint, we'd haul out some idea (figuring we had the kid this time!) and say *Then why don't you do* this or that? Then the complaining kid would say triumphantly, *Naw, I don't want to! Well, what about doing* this or that other thing, we'd say, and the kid would say *Uh-uh,* and then we'd say *O.K., what about . . .* and the kid got to say *No Good* and then cut out and go to the bathroom and arrive back later saying *There's Nothing Going On.*

This drove us out of our minds, and it drove us out of our minds every day. We tried to figure it out, and couldn't do it. All we could see was that the fucking kids were trying to drive us out of our minds. We did see that somehow this was the crucial issue of the course. Unaccountably, the course was not, as we'd thought, a course where students would get to do all the things we'd thought up for them to do, but instead a course where they could steadfastly refuse to do everything and then complain that there was nothing to do.

Christopher Columbus schemed and made a lot of plans and talked the principal into it and finally set sail for India, figuring that if he could get there by this new route he would become rich and famous. Unfortunately he ran into the New World first. Columbus' plans were all predicated on it being India, so he didn't know what to do with it, didn't understand it, and ended up convinced that everyone was trying to drive him out of his mind.

Since there weren't going to be any spices or silks, he became obsessed with the only thing left to insure riches and fame. He thus tortured Carib and Arawak chiefs from all over, figuring from Old World premises that they knew where the gold was but naturally wouldn't tell him. It never penetrated his mind that they really didn't have any. Columbus sailed North and South and East, gold and the Old World reinforcing a vertical logic which prevented him from sailing West long enough to actually run into gold.

On one of his sailing trips, he came across several very large canoes, way out of sight of land. The canoes seemed to be full of richly dressed native businessmen, all painted and befeathered and going somewhere definite and purposive. But Columbus knew that the natives of the New World didn't go out of sight of land. He mentioned them in dispatches as an oddity, something else trying to drive him out of his mind, intimated that they were crazy, and forgot them. He didn't try to find out where they lived, or where they were going. He didn't follow them, or torture them, or try to get rich and famous from them. They didn't fit into his notion of how things were, didn't make any sense in view of his idea of what he was doing. It was too bad. I don't think Columbus ever found out that those seagoing businessmen were most likely Aztecs, possessors in nearby Mexico City of all the gold in the world. Columbus invented the New World, but its terms lay apart from his Old World logic and he just couldn't take any advantage from it.

Frank and I did a little better than Columbus. If we never quite accepted the notion that the real curriculum of the course was precisely the question What Shall We Do In Here? and that it was really an important question and maybe the only important question, we did finally understand that there was no gold in CA. We did see that if you agreed beforehand not to threaten the kids with grades, and if you agreed that everyone could leave the room at any time without asking you, that you had just entered a New World.

But quite late in the year, we did get some idea of where we were. There was a big blond kid named Greg in the class, and Greg had maddened us all year. He wouldn't do anything at all, he complained all the time about there was nothing to do, he scoffed at all our ideas, he gave the finger to Egypt classes every day, he Took Advantage Of Freedom, he smoked in the bathroom, he encouraged Marcia and Mike Hunt, he was the original big lump of a thirteen-year-old in a canoe way out of sight of land, just trying to drive us crazy. That goddamn purposeless Greg, Frank and I often told each other, thinking frankly that if we could just get rid of him, transfer him out into some other class, then things might go right . . . Well, one day the roof finally fell in on Greg and he reaped the rewards of all his fucking around all year. The counselors, taking note of all his F's and Unsatisfactories for Citizenship, sent out forms to his teachers, asking them to comment. Of course they all wrote that he was no damn good. So the counselors called his parents and they had to come in, and there they were with the principal and the vice-principal and the counselors and the teachers and there was Greg, faced with all those adults come to deal with the fact that he was no good. There in the office, hearing all the teachers tell Greg's parents that he wouldn't do Spelling, wouldn't do Science, wouldn't do this and that (wouldn't even do Shop, for Christ's sake!), in the face of all those helpful, frowning adults, Frank and I suddenly saw that Greg was really O.K. We remembered that he always helped out collating the magazine; we remembered he'd gotten the ladder and fixed up the lights for the play I'd insisted on putting on; we remembered that he always knew how many kids were in each class when we needed to know in order to distribute *Infinity;* we remembered that he'd helped Piston carry the kite down to the field, and we just remembered that he was usually around when something really needed to be done—in short, we all of a sudden realized that he was a pretty helpful, alert, responsible kid, and we said so. Everyone was astonished.

Could he spell? Did he do Egypt? Did he make book ends? We insisted. He was an O.K. kid. We convinced ourselves because we knew it was true. It was a big step for us. We left realizing that we had just realized that this fuck-up kid who drove us crazy was really O.K. and that, far from the class being better if he was gotten rid of, he was actually needed in CA. Therefore, we had to admit, in some way, somehow, our New World class was O.K. too. I mean, if the most fucked-up kid in the class was O.K., as we quite clearly *felt* he was O.K. (although our Old World logic told us he wasn't), and if we were willing to say out loud that he was O.K., if we were going to tell his parents that their kid was O.K. . . . well, it means that even if we had to admit we weren't going to find gold, that anyway discovering the New World was something in itself, and was probably enough for us to do that year. Frank and I came out of the meeting looking at each other strangely, wondering what had happened to us.

Chapter IV

Creative Arts

I'm sure it was during that very year, sometime
in the spring, that certain shocking photographs
began to come to the attention of the staff. These pictures
all were alike in one respect—they showed a naked
youthful male figure from about bellybutton to mid-thigh.
Beyond that general likeness, each was different, of course.
Lots of pubic hair, or scanty pubic hair, or in between—
dark or medium or light (the photos were not in color).
Very definite suntan lines, or medium, or none. Con-
voluted or spiral or just plain indented bellybuttons. Then
the dicks—circumcised or uncircumcised to begin with,
long and skinny, or short and fat, or long and fat, or
short and skinny, or medium-sized "average" dicks.

What was it all about. Well, while Frank and I were
trying to get the kids to do something creative, the kids
invented a little art of their own. Boys cut out from
school, during lunchtime or perhaps after school or even
before school, down to the Tierra Firma Shopping
Center where there was a photomat machine and booth.
For a quarter you could get your picture taken. So instead
of sitting there grinning into the lens with your hair all
combed, you pulled down your pants and shorts, pulled
up your shirt and stood up on the seat while a confeder-
ate shoved in a quarter and others stood outside making
sure no one came around. It was all done in a split second

and then you all had those photos. At school these could be given to others who would then be able to pass them around to the girls. The passing around had to be complicated enough so that no one knew who was who (often the kid himself didn't know any more whether that particular bellybutton, pubic hair and dick was himself or someone else) and then the girls could try to guess who was who, or what was who?

You can see the virtue—the creativeness, I ought to add—in this whole thing. I mean, once a girl even looked like she might try to guess, she was involved in a terrible admission. If she disdained the gambit, it was an admission of another sort too. Besides, who can resist guessing? The best thing was that there was no danger involved, since no one knew any longer whose picture it was anyway.

Frank and I heard about it through Piston. *Some other kids,* he told us, were doing that, taking those pictures. He made us promise not to tell any other teachers, but in fact shortly afterwards they all knew about it. They knew about it because kids told them, or made sure the pictures were passed around in the room where the teacher would have to see them, try to ignore them as she might. Some arts cannot complete their virtue until they are exposed to the enemy.

The teachers were upset about this degeneracy, of course, but I think they were tickled too. It never became the subject of faculty meetings, for instance, like the dull sins of gum chewing and running in the halls. After a short time, some of the girls (no doubt those who had done the guessing) began to show up with their own pictures. These showed, at the top, two hands holding a pulled up sweater or blouse, below that two twelve- or thirteen-year-old breasts and below that an uncertain expanse of skin and occasionally a bellybutton. But at the same time the school went into action in a kind of underground way, i.e., not by faculty meetings or sending mimeographed letters home to alert the community or anything of that sort, but only by talking and laughing with itself until it finally talked and laughed to the vice-principal, who then had to go down at lunchtime and stand around in front of the photomat as the school knew he would have to do and would do and that was the end of the activity.

It had lasted long enough—two or three weeks, just about the same time as a school play or art festival or any other creative school endeavor. I doubt anyone was unhappy when it was over. Two or three days were profitably spent in talk about it, complaining happily about the Up-Tight vice-principal who wouldn't let anyone do anything they wanted to do and about the cowardice of the girls who were afraid to photograph their cunts, while the girls retorted that (1) it was just too bad the boys didn't have nothing up above to show and (2) the boys must be pretty ignorant of the location of cunts if they thought there was any way to take pictures of them in that photomat.

Occasionally during the rest of the year such pictures as hadn't been confiscated or lost or hidden secretly away at home showed up in class. Then there would be a bit of an uproar, some grabbing, the same innuendo about guessing, and then someone would say *Remember that?* and everyone would remember it and all about it as a bit of history and good old times that year in the seventh or eighth grade at Spanish Main Intermediate School.

34

Chapter V

Return of } The Hawk
Son of {

One Sunday afternoon towards the end of the
year Frank and I went one step further. At the
time we didn't know or care that we were going One
Step Further—that is only how I see it now. We were
up in the country having a picnic and talking along the
way about movies and it occurred to us that you could
make a movie very well at a school and we began to
make it up. We made up an entire movie then and there
and since Frank knew about cameras and film and since
he had a Sears and Roebuck movie camera we made up
our minds to do it. We figured out a great script about a
mad kid who murders everyone in a school.

The only thing I had to offer was a marvelous Hawk
mask which a painter had made for Jay one Halloween.
We decided to use that mask as the main image of the
movie—the costume the murderous kid would put on
when he felt murderous. See, he would be a respectable
kid, Student-Body President perhaps, whose daddy or older brother or something (I forget) would have been The
Hawk a while back and killed a lot of people and then
disappeared, but the kid remembered. No one else knew
about it or knew that the kid's father or brother had been
The Hawk.

Frank and I showed up at school on Monday feeling great. Were we planning to suggest to the kids in CA *How About Making A Film?* and hear them say No We Don't Want To, or There's Nothing To Do Around Here, and then we'd try to persuade them into it and they'd say Have You Seen Mike Hunt? Hell no. It never occurred to us to wonder whether they wanted to make a film at all. We wanted to make a film ourselves and spend the rest of the year doing it. We didn't want to find out what the kids' notions of films were. We didn't want to see what they would do with the film. We didn't want to inspect their creativity.

Had we wanted to See What The Kids Would Do With Film, we'd have no doubt come up with something more constructive—a film about Attitudes And Relationships or The Question Of Authority and/or Democracy In The Classroom . . . as it was, we really wanted to make a Tarzan film but couldn't quite see how it could be done and settled for The Hawk.

Let me make the point, before I forget it and breeze on, remembering the movie. If, in the New World, the role of the teacher as giver of orders didn't work out (no one had to follow them orders) it was also true that the other role (the one Frank and I had imagined)—the teacher as Provider Of Things To Do, the teacher as Entertainer—didn't work out either. For wasn't that just what the kids had been telling us all year in their oblique, exasperating way? What did all that Nothing To Do In Here mean, if not that the kids didn't want entertainers, wouldn't accept them if they didn't have to, wanted the teachers to be something else entirely?

Wanted them to be what? What was the difference between all the grand things we'd thought up for the kids to do and The Hawk? Why, merely that we didn't want to do any of the former ourselves and we did want to do the latter. Why should we have assumed that the kids would want to do a lot of stuff that we didn't want to do, wouldn't ever do of our own free will? It sounds nonsensical, put that way. Yet that is the assumption under which I operated, Frank operated, for many a year, under which almost all teachers operate, and it is idiotic. (Does the math teacher go home at night and do a few magic squares? Does the English teacher go home and analyze sentences? Does the reading teacher turn off the TV and drill herself on syllables and Reading Comprehension? Or do any of us do any of those things, even in the classroom?)

Wanted them to be human. Men. Wanted them to define themselves. (Do I define myself as a person who writes fake Peace Corps journals?) Wanted them to stick by Harry Sullivan's rule: Human beings are more alike than not. What you don't do, we probably don't want to do. What you learn from, we probably learn from.

We fired right off on Monday afternoon with the movie. Our main location was the tennis courts next to the field below the school. It was a huge field of grass which was never used by anyone except for girls' PE for softball, two or three weeks out of the year, although the school was overcrowded. Everyone complained about the fact that the other field—the one the kids were allowed to use —was too crowded to play on; at the same time everyone decided not to allow the kids to use the field in question because they would have to be supervised and that would double the duty for teachers and that was out of the question. No one used the tennis courts either, except for the girls' PE about three weeks out of the year and some teachers who played once in a while after school. We went down, Frank and I, seventh period to those tennis courts; a bunch of kids and I watched while Frank filmed the lines running up and down the court very artistically and then I chalked the title *Son of The Hawk* or *Return of The Hawk* (I really don't remember which it was) on the green cement and Frank filmed that and also the legend *A C-Arts Production*. Part of Frank's seventh period class watched too (it was either Social Studies or English) and the rest were—where? It was the same with my own eighth period class who were told by me to either come watch or get into the film or just stay in the room . . . The Hawk made us irresponsible.

By then a lot of kids wanted to be in the film and a lot didn't. We picked who was to be who and divulged the plot. A lot of kids wanted to know why we wanted to call it *Return of The Hawk* (or *Son of*) but we didn't really care to explain. We knew they hadn't seen all them old movies so how were they to know? We were pleased to be authoritarian. Everyone picked a tall, handsome, vain kid named Jon to be the hero and we agreed, mainly because the name was right. We picked Jane to be the heroine; we picked Harvey to be The Hawk, since he was the only one who was brave enough to say he wanted to be The Hawk. We picked Jane, by the way, because she had done all that work all year long and we liked her and because she admitted she wanted to be the heroine. We would have picked Meg and Lily too, except that they said they didn't want to be in the movie. They had other things to do and would be satisfied with bit parts when they weren't busy.

The movie opened. Julie (Jane) and Jon came down the steps holding hands, carrying tennis rackets. They paused for a kiss. Then they went down and started play-ing tennis. They played a bit. Cut to the fence; a terrible claw (which Jane had spent some time making out of an old rubber glove and cardboard fingernails and green and red paint) was seen shoving a green tennis ball through the fence and rolling it towards the players. The camera followed it rolling along so everyone would know it was important. Show Julie picking up ball and talking. Cut to title which I chalked on the green cement: Oh look, Jon, a green tennis ball! Show Julie holding ball. Then show Julie's hand turning green. Some kid paints Julie's hand a little bit with green paint, Frank films it, the kid paints a little more, he films that—pretty soon Julie's whole arm is green! It is a poison ball! Oh Jon! calls out Julie, and falls over dead. Over by the fence, for a brief instant, the shadow of the hawk mask, then legs running up the stairs. The legs have red tennis shoes on, painted up beforehand. Jon runs over and sees Julie is dead, grinning into the camera all the time.

About that time Frank decided to wait for the "rushes" before shooting any more. When the film was developed and we showed ourselves those rushes, the film became a movie and became real. Everyone saw where the movie was headed, several kids wanted to make suggestions about what to do next, two kids wanted to be cameramen, and everyone wanted to be in it. So that the next day when we started again, there was Jon grinning and saying Poor Julie's dead! and suddenly hundreds (it seemed) of cops rushed from everywhere. There were three authentic cops' jackets and a number of detectives in long raincoats and dark glasses (one leading a dachshund on a leash)—there were also two new cameramen. They filmed Jon, suddenly afraid the cops would think he did it, running to hide in a garbage can, from which half of him stuck out. They filmed the cops and detectives combing the school, climbing over the fences, investigating the office (the principal might have done it!) and Piston as detective snooping around the girls' bathrooms. They took off and filmed The Hawk making an obscure phone call from a booth at the gas station down by the shopping center—the purpose of the call not clear, except for the fact that everyone concerned got to leave the school grounds, and all the kids who watched the movie (they realized that it was a real movie and people would be coming to see it) would know they'd left the school grounds.

Next The Hawk was shown in the darkened science room, mask on, preparing his deadly green poison. Everyone volunteered to smoke cigarettes to produce clouds of smoke and an air of mystery. The Hawk was shown pulling out a lot of junk from an old closet, including an old newspaper, mocked-up by Jane (now, as Julie, dead, and reverting to make-up and prop manager) which told about the old Hawk; the present Hawk swore revenge.

Well, anyway, the plot changed entirely from our original Sunday afternoon conception. It turned out The Hawk's motivation was that he loved the girl Julie, who didn't love him, in spite of the fact he was Student-Body President, but instead that damn conceited Jon. The Hawk had sworn to get her, psychologically twisted as he was, it was implied, by memory of his criminal relative. So there was a lot of panic in the school. Shots showing girls screaming, kids whispering in class (Who is The Hawk?), teachers trying to calm things down, and a splendid burst of paper airplanes flying around and landing to show the legend Watch Out For The Hawk! or The Hawk Is Coming! Hordes of girl reporters besieged the principal (Lou, in dark glasses, was persuaded to look outraged) and he was quoted as saying If we catch The Hawk, he'll be Suspended! Vern the counselor looked serious and allowed as how The Hawk wasn't very well adjusted, or something like that. Julie's mother and father (two kids with Jane-produced gray hair and a mustache) tearfully and cheerfully said We told her not to play with boys! All the time there were shots of those giveaway red tennis shoes walking around here and there, unsuspected.

Frank and I had been edged out as director and cameraman and organizer without any fuss. While everyone had talked about what ought to happen, during the rushes a boy named Phil had written it down and produced a "shooting schedule." He directed from then on because he wanted to direct and knew how to say "shooting schedule." The two cameramen took over as cameramen for the same reasons—they wanted to be, could do it, and did it. The director consulted with Frank, and the cameramen recognized my lust to become a cameraman (never having taken so much as a Brownie photo in my life and afraid of doing so now, while actually dying to) and showed me this and that and let me film a few scenes. Certain kids took over the chalking up of speeches on the tennis court. Other kids took over the organization of crowds when we needed them, bursting into classes and saying We need a crowd! (No one ever

40

suggested filming crowd scenes during lunch, when no classes would have to be interrupted.) Seventh and eighth periods became the time when *The Hawk* was being filmed; the other school considerations—passes, grades, authority, work or not-work, There's Nothing To Do, narcs, complaints—were forgotten. Frank and I, talking things over, found ourselves pleased—not that the Class was going well, but that the Film was going well. When it rained, we all just sat around the classroom content and relaxed, doing nothing without anxiety about doing nothing or should we be doing Nothing or Something or how to tell our parents we weren't doing nothing? and was it educationally sound to do nothing? . . . for we weren't doing nothing. but instead we were sitting around waiting for the rain to stop. It is a big difference.

Well, there were a few shots of Jon, who'd been hiding out from the cops, sneaking around the school trying to find out who The Hawk was. Finally he got into the science room one (simulated) night, and discovered the mask and claws and poison and the old newspapers, hidden away in a cardboard box in a cabinet. Then he knew (reading the name of The Hawk's old man or brother) and there was a dramatic smoke-filled shot of him smearing the Hawk mask with the green poison, grinning into the camera all the time. Phil was upset by now with all that grinning and vanity, but couldn't stop it and there was nothing to be done about it. The next scene showed a poster announcing a Memorial Assembly For Julie and a lot of kids standing around it, girls crying . . . all of this working up to the grand finale.

We filled the multi-use room with kids. Up on the stage came Harvey, the Student-Body President. He began to lead the salute to the flag. All the kids stood up. Cut to his feet. He's wearing red tennis shoes! ". . . with liberty and justice for all," says the title on the green cement. Everyone sits down. Jon gets up in the audience. He comes up to the stage, carrying a cardboard box wrapped with a big ribbon. He presents it to the President. The President is astonished. "For me?" he says. He opens it,

41

unsuspecting. Out of the box he pulls the Hawk mask! His look turns to anger and hatred. Driven mad, he puts on the mask and shakes his fist at the audience. *The Hawk! Our President's The Hawk!* yell some kids. Shots of girls screaming. Then, *Get him!* shout the kids, and the Hawk leaps off the stage. Shots of The Hawk running out of the multi-use room, shots of the crowd chasing him, the last movement of Brahms' Fourth blasting away (later—on tape I mean, at the premiere—I finally got to do something). We had to retake that scene many times because the crowd kept catching The Hawk before he got out the door. They caught him and tackled him and mobbed him over and over again. Fuck this! yelled The Hawk finally, shoving kids off him, these dumb ass-holes are trying to really kill me! Finally he gets out and flees around the school and then down the steps to the field and the tennis courts, the crowd hot after him. A lot of tricky stuff with speeding up the camera and slow motion. Close-ups of the mask, showing it turning green. Harvey is marvelous; we are all amazed. Staggering, jerking, almost falling (the poison is getting to him), shaking his fist, running in circles, on and on the scene goes, piling up like Brahms . . . he finally collapses in slow motion. The crowd comes up, also in slow motion. Jon reaches down and pulls off the mask. The Hawk's face is green. He is dead. The crowd's fury is over. All look sad. The tape changes to Miles Davis playing "My Funny Valentine." Girls cry. Miles sounds regretful. Everyone starts to go. Jon is all alone with the dead Hawk. The cameramen have learned not to focus on his face, but now it can't be helped. He looks into the camera, grins, and says, "My best friend!" Then he sits down, takes off his shoes and puts on the red tennis shoes. Long shot from above the field, the tennis courts empty except for the dead Hawk, the sitting Jon. Miles plays out the tape to the end.

We put on a grand premiere. We had posters all over, giving the stars' names, the credits; we dittoed off cards for audience reaction, set up chairs in the music room, a white elephant of a building, round without windows, which had been built by some smart architect and which looked modern and which was useless for everything. It was just right for a movie. We showed *The Hawk* over and over, to a hundred kids at a time, watched every showing ourselves, and felt superior to everyone. We spent the rest of the year doing that, and talking about the movie among ourselves when we weren't showing it. We'd spent about two months making it; it was exactly twenty-two and a half minutes long; it had cost just slightly over twenty-five dollars. We asked ourselves just why it was that the hero put on the red tennis shoes at the end? Was he going to turn into another Hawk? Was it just some kind of sentimental gesture? We didn't know. All we remembered was that there at the end someone had called out Put on his shoes! and everyone had felt that was right and so Jon had done it. It was pointed out that no one in the audience had ever asked about it, and so it must be just right, even if we didn't know why.

Chapter VI

A Dog at School

Dogs often wander into the classrooms at schools, and always cause an uproar. Kids cannot contain themselves when dogs appear in the midst of Egypt lesson, for what reason no one seems to know. Why couldn't they, the kids, just let the dog be in the class, wandering around, sniffing here and licking a few hands there, quietly, moseying about in the style of dogs while the class continued with the most important part of the lesson about Egypt? But no, they can't. They got to rush the dog, they got to pick him up and drop him, they got to offer the dog candy and pieces of sandwich, they got to yell and scream and act like they never saw any dog before in their whole lives. So the teacher then got to say Get that dog out of here! (saying later in the teachers' room, *I* don't mind the dog, I even *got* a dog at home and *like* dogs, and if those kids could just have the dog in there without all that fussing during the crucial lesson about Egypt when I just *got* to get it over to them, what's the problem? haven't they ever seen a dog before?) and nine kids got to chase the dog around until the teacher got to grab the dog herself and throw the dog out and shut the door and then argue with the kids about having the dog in the room (if you could just *have* the dog and not have to make such a commotion, she says to them, trying to explain, not wanting to be some kind of monster, hating dogs, while all they want is that *dog*).

What's it all about? Well, of course, that dog is alive, and old Egypt is dead. That's not crucial to all kids, you know. Some kids like Egypt a lot and eat up all the Egypt books the library has got, which is plenty. I can easily imagine Piston right now (it is several years since I have seen Piston) reading The Book of the Dead with great concentration (stubbornness) while every dog in the world licks his feet and tries to play and eat his sandwich. Piston doesn't even know them dogs are around, for he has got other things to do, namely make his way through the underworld.

Outside Smiley's Bar and Bait Shop in Bolinas there lives and operates a fabulous, obsessed dog. Bolinas, by the way, is probably the dog capital of the world. There are dogs everywhere—lying in the streets, cluttering up the gas station, sniffing the baits of fishermen, roaming the beaches, trying to get in the grocery store, waiting for people at the post office—everywhere you go there are plenty of dogs. They are all big dogs, all are friendly, all wag their tails, all hope for handouts—they are, in short, good dogs and everyone in Bolinas digs them, I think.

The dog outside Smiley's is a German shepherd of uncertain age. Not young, anyway. A bit scraggly, thin of hair on the back, long in the tooth as they say. Someone owns him; I'm not sure who. It wasn't until about the middle of August that I noticed him. Of course, as I emerge from Smiley's I am a bit foggy in the mind and not apt to notice much; I am heading for the pier to see what's happening with Jay and Jack and the pink or rose-tailed perch or the once-in-a-lifetime rubber-lip. I noticed him because one day he came into Smiley's. There he dropped an old gray tattered tennis ball between his paws and waited, looking intently at the ball. As no one made a move, he backed off from it a bit, six inches at the most. By then everyone at the bar was looking at him. Jerry came out from behind the bar and made a grab for the ball. Quick as a wink, the dog snatched it up;

immediately, he let it down again, right between his paws. Jerry moved slightly, a feint. The dog didn't move. Then he grabbed for it, and the dog snatched it with his jaws. He let it down again. No one seemed disposed to try to get it. He moved back, moved back again, edged just a bit farther back. Jerry was back behind the bar. I inquired. That's all he does, all day, and maybe all night, ever'day, said Jerry. That's his thing, and he does it. I drank some beer and got down off the bar stool to try him out. Edged toward the ball. Moved. The dog's jaws had it before I got close. He dropped it again. I moved for it. He had it. Dropped it. Moved. Snap. Drop. Moved . . . me, a new man, playing ball, everyone watching a minor event in the beginning of the day. I went back to my beer. About the time I was ready to leave, an old lady, drunk as a coot at ten in the morning, got off her stool and said so long to Jerry. She ambled down the bar, heading for the door. As she got alongside the dog she suddenly launched out with a tremendous kick at the grimy tennis ball on the floor. It was beautiful. Her shoe touched the ball just as the dog's jaw fastened on it. She fell on her ass with a tremendous roar of laughter and the dog stood up with the ball just barely clasped in his jaws at the very edge—a close thing, a tie, a standoff between equals. The old lady got up and gave the dog a big salute as she went out. The dog, satisfied perhaps, went out too.

Every day after that I looked for the dog. I introduced Jay and Jack to him. He played with them indulgently like an old hero hitting fungoes to the rookies. I saw him every day, at all hours of the day, and he always had the tennis ball, and he always had it there between his paws, or had backed off a foot or so from it, giving the whole world a chance if it thought it was good enough, staring down with the utmost concentration (stubbornness) at that ball, not questioning the fact that the world was as interested in it as he was.

One morning I came out of Smiley's and there he was in the middle of the street. There was nothing extraordinary about the day. No omens, signs or portents. I was just heading for the pier, having drunk a couple of beers and read the sports page. The dog had left the ball a good foot and a half from his jaws, recognizing in me an inept player, hoping to entice me into a grab. Well, I was game, and approached. As I poised foggily for a snatch, a tremendous uproar of barking came from behind the dog. A great gang of other dogs had apparently discovered something intolerable about the state of affairs of the world and begun an outcry. The old obsessed dog, startled, re-entered the real world of dogs for the first time in years, just long enough to turn his head one split second—the splittest of split seconds—and did so just as I grabbed, by luck, and when he turned back to The Book of the Dead I had it in the back pocket of my Levi's and was standing there innocently looking up at the sky to see if it might rain. Lord have mercy! That dog's head turned nine ways at once, and then he jumped straight up in the air, came down, looked everywhere, up, down, sideways, in back, rushed into the bar, came out, searched one side of the street and then the other, turned around on his axis, examined the sky, scratched the ground, implored heaven, yelped piteously, barked, snarled . . . Terrified, I took out the tennis ball and (not having received any Gold Medal, which I deserved) gave it a toss down the road so he'd have to chase it. He did. Got it, brought it back, let it down between his paws, backed off, staring at it intently. Nothing was going to change, whether heaven willed it or not. I see it, said Jerry from the door of Smiley's, but I don't believe it! Of course I knew it was only luck, and the dog knew it was only some inexplicable jest of the gods, so neither of us was much affected; in fact we just went on with our lives as if nothing had happened at all.

But it goes to show that you have got to be obsessed to drag your real life into Egypt and The Book of the Dead (in fact I have never heard of any junior high school Egypt teachers bringing in The Book of the Dead to their classes, dog-ridden or not), and even then, even for the obsessed, anything real and alive coming into your classroom like a dog or a bee or a monstrous kite is bound to claim your attention if only for a split second. And if you are not obsessed (and there are still many of us who are not, believe it if you can) then you have simply got to throw books at the real, feed the real sandwiches, murder the real, at least glance for that split second at the real, no matter what the subsequent cost— be it loss of tennis ball or note home for unsatisfactory attention and work habits.

Chapter VII

An Environment for Lizards

Last year we never had a lizard in the room. This year, right now, we have thirteen. Last year Tizzo and Junior and Karl occasionally wanted to go out and *hunt for lizards* but they never brought any back, which was because what they really wanted to do was get off the school grounds, smoke and be free. It was only some errant folk memory which made them think of lizards as an excuse in the first place. Occasionally they brought back a sow bug or a worm, to show they were serious. They ain't got lizards around here like they used to, they told me.

This year seven boys showed up the second day with lizards. Give you curriculum planners cause to reflect.

They have these lizards arranged in an aquarium full of dirt, rocks, some dried-up ice plant, an old abalone shell and a tin with water in it. From day to day there are also different pieces of clay, sculptured into tunnels and caves for the lizards to hide in. Alas, there is no hiding, for also in the aquarium at all times are five or six pairs of hands, busily rearranging and resculpturing the lizards' Heimat, taking out the lizards, making more devious and restful tunnels and caves, rebuilding the rock grottoes, putting the lizards back in, digging up, smoothing out the dirt, taking out the lizards again, pouring in a load of sand from the jumping pit . . . no harm is meant to the lizards, in fact everyone is quite solicitous, buying meal worms for them, hoping to see them lose their skin, yelling at each other to be careful . . .

Well, it is bugging me, all right. I approach for a subtle talk. Careful to compliment the lizards, for which Richard has made signs stuck in the dirt, saying Blue-belly and Alligator, I try out the idea that maybe the lizards would like to be left in peace. The hands are busy in the dirt as I speak. Everyone agrees. They are trying to make the lizards happier by making tunnels and caves to rest in and to hide in, I'm told. Of course. I bring up the notion that in the lizards' natural environment (I say) it is an odd but true fact that hands are not digging them new holes every day, not making interesting new rock formations, not unloading tons of sand making it nine different levels like Troy but that in fact they have quite a while to get used to and make use of whatever ground they (for whatever reason) end up in. Everyone agrees. For instance, I add, you guys found them lizards under the ice plant, and if everyone didn't keep digging up the ice plant, maybe it would grow and—everyone agrees. They tell each other to quit digging up the place. All hands are busy inside the aquarium. In short, I say, why not leave them awhile to the present highly adequate arrangement? Them lizards (I say) won't ever have time to grow a new skin at this rate. They'll be too busy exploring. Right? Right. The lizards are jerked out so they'll be out of the way of a new freeway; they lie stunned on the counter next to the sink. Back in they go. Everyone advises everyone else to leave them alone and not keep on messing with them. One lizard's tail is painted blue. Everyone watches to see if they will crawl into the new holes, but no one can wait and fingers prod them along. Lots of advice about leaving them alone. Mr. Herndon is right, you guys!

Leave them alone then, I want to say. Out come the lizards. In go some more rocks.

Then leave them alone for a while, goddamnit! I do say, loudly. Everyone looks at me in astonishment.

My wife Fran goes to visit Tierra Firma Elementary

School, where our kids go, one morning and ends up staying the day. She is appalled at the playground scene. It appears that the kids (kindergarten to sixth grade) are all running around yelling about *kill* and *murder* and *beat up* and about *stupid* and *MR* and *dumb-ass* and two kids are holding another kid while a third socks him in the belly (it happens to be Jay, our oldest, who is getting socked) and two little white kids are refusing to let a bigger black kid play football with them and so the black kid starts to beat them up and when the playground woman comes over they all three give her a lot of shit and run away and she can't catch them . . . another large group of kids are playing dodge ball and throwing the ball hard and viciously at one another's heads, and some of them are crying, and other kids wander around crying, and there is a whole other population of kids who stand fearfully on the outskirts of the grounds just trying to keep out of the way . . .

Back in the classroom after lunch she observes the concerned teachers trying to have some discussion with the kids about how to treat other people, about violence, about calling names—suddenly, says Fran, they are all these goddamn nice neat marvelous white middle-class children, even if occasionally black, talking about equal rights and observing the rights of others and not giving way to vagrant impulse and how war is bad and everyone is smart (even them fucking MR's) and how in a democracy everyone must be responsible for his or her own actions. They all know what to say! hollers Fran to me. They have all the words! They discuss superbly. They are a veritable UN of kids, schooled in the right phrase, diplomatic, unctuous, tolerant, fair . . . the hypocritical little bastards! Sucking up, that's what they are! And believing it at the same time! Talk is cheap!

No doubt. It is the original prerogative of the white American middle class to be sucking up while at the same time actually believing everything it says. Lizards can tell you all about it.

51

Chapter VIII

The Stream of Life

Frank and I promptly abandoned the New World.
Or the school abandoned it. In fact, both parties
agreed. One of the factors was that Lou quit as principal
and farmed himself out to pasture at San Francisco State.
Well, he had been there two years, and that was par.
But the new principal happened to be the very same man
who had pulled his son out of CA within three or four
weeks after school began, telling Frank that he didn't intend to have his kid in a class where you didn't learn
nothing. There was the fact that Frank and the new
principal had some long-standing grudge against each
other, and Frank didn't intend to be working some class
where the kids would be running around the place and
that principal would get to complain to him about his
students. There was the fact that Frank had been teaching
about ten years in junior high school (as I have now)
and he was just plain weary of it. He wanted to spend
his days by himself, for a change, to think and write and
go to the track.

There was also the astonishing fact that the school as
a whole showed no signs of wanting to enter the New
World, or even to recognize it. The most positive re-
sponse to CA among the faculty was from people who
figured Frank and I had figured out a way to goof off
and not-teach—the more general opinion was that CA

52

encouraged other kids to wonder why they couldn't do nothing too, couldn't have Permanent Hall Passes, and thus that it was an undesirable element of sabotage. CA, of course, continued to exist. Once something is started in a school, it is not easily given up, no matter if anyone likes it or not. It became the province of the drama teacher. The justification for keeping it was that it gave the students a wider choice of electives, which naturally meant that if they didn't like Drama they could take CA, which turned out to be just like Drama. I had really decided that you couldn't have the New World for one class a day. It would have to be all or nothing; I planned to agitate for the all.

Summer came. We went up camping on the Trinity River. Mainly we went there because I was certain I would catch a steelhead in that river. We traveled the length of the river from the coast to Weaverville, passing up camping places because they were too gravelly or had trailers or looked like state parks or because we wanted to go on and see what the next one looked like, and finally ended up at a place called Big Bar where there was a forest service camp with room enough for only three camps and there we called it a day. It was a wonderful place with huge yellow pines on the edge of a creek overgrown with brush and those bright leafy small trees through which sunlight filters and glitters. The powerful Trinity rushed past at the foot of the hill. Jay roamed the place in his Levi jacket and black cowboy boots. Jack, six weeks old or so, lay on his back on a blanket. When we arrived a guy and his family were just leaving, having just spent one day. Plenty of trout in the creek, he told me. You can't help catch them. Down at the store, a mile or two away, the owner, George, told me, Plenty of steelhead in the river. We went out to the high bridge there and looked over, and sure enough there were the steelhead lying back of the boulders and in the pools. Actually I might have thought those steelhead were sunken logs or just shadows, but George knew all about it. Well,

53

I put in several eight-hour days working on that river without ever catching a steelhead. I worked overtime on the creek, catching about one small trout an hour. On the other hand, if I went down to the great river with Jay and if we stood out in the river (chest high for Jay who had to stand in front of me to avoid being swept off his feet), we caught all the trout in the world, although George assured us you couldn't catch no trout in the river at this time of year. We kept going over to the store, where every day I would see these two big steelhead in the ice-chest. No matter how often I asked when and by whom those steelhead were caught I couldn't ever get a straight answer from George, and in fact I came to the conclusion that these two big steelhead were mummies, but just the same I'd talk with George about catching steelhead and buy a Mepps Spinner of a different size or color or a couple of salmon flies or some night crawlers or whatever George said you could be sure to catch steelhead on today. Then Jay and I would get a beer and a 7-Up and go sit outside on the bench and George would blow up a balloon inside and bring it out and secretly rub it against his chest and then stick it on Jay's head. Well the balloon would stick there; Jay was astonished every time. Old Glue-head! George would cry. He was as astonished as Jay, it seemed. You must have got glue on yore head, he'd tell Jay. Jay knew he didn't have no glue on his head, because we didn't have any glue. Still, how did that balloon stick there? Maybe you got some of that pine pitch, George would suggest. Jay always felt that might be it, since he had that ole pine pitch all over every other part of him. He'd feel his head and try to discover pine pitch, and sometimes he thought yeah, he did feel a little pine pitch up there and sometimes he thought no, he didn't feel any.

When I got back the school had a new program. The junior high school assumes that it was invented in order to bridge the gap between elementary and high school, but it is always uncertain which way it ought to lean. In our case, Spanish Main had started out leaning toward the elementary side, but by the time I got there it was definitely taking a hard line toward high school, telling the kids stuff like you have to grow up, take responsibility, get along with more than one teacher. But over that summer someone had had second thoughts, it seemed, and recognized that in the school there were a number of kids who didn't take to the hard-line high school approach. It was decided to call these kids "immature" and deal with them in a self-contained classroom, for one year, "to make their transition easier." There were only a couple such classes. Apparently the one thousand or so other kids weren't immature.

It seems to me now that that was the beginning (at SM) of two tactics used by public schools to win their battle for existence; first, to establish special groups of kids in various categories ranging from "immature" through neurologically or emotionally or educationally "handicapped" to "deprived" to the marvelous, blatant "non-achiever," and second, to take teachers who wish to teach in some odd way and let them teach those odd kids. For all the terms for special kids really just mean kids who can't or won't or don't do things the way the school thinks they ought to be done; once labeled as special, the school can pretend that there is a *normal* group which is well served by the custom of the school. The school's obvious inability to satisfy many children can then become natural, since the kids are "special" and *shouldn't* be satisfied by any normal procedures and the school does not need to change its ways at all, has only to create some arrangements on the outskirts of the school to keep them special kids and special teachers out of the way.

I wasn't thinking of that at the time. Frankly, the first few days I was besieged by parents who wanted to know if their kids were in some sort of dumb class. What the parents instinctively knew was that any special arrangement probably meant the school considered their kids to be dumb or goofy, and in any case, didn't think they would be going to Harvard. They wanted to know how their kids happened to get in this class and they wanted it understood that their kids weren't dumb, and if it *was* a dumb class they wanted their kids out of it and promised to cooperate by making them do homework, forbidding TV, and so on. Well, I ended up telling the parents what the school told me, which was that the kids were supposed to be "immature" rather than dumb, that in fact they were probably a brighter group than most, that the school was not selling them out of Harvard, and in any case I wasn't. That satisfied almost everyone. Immaturity was O.K. with them.

I tried to think then why it was that these kids were supposed by the school to be immature. Now, I decide to isolate the quality of stubbornness. I know that it is only in terms of the book that I say so. It is simply that the kids as I remember them demonstrated no other particular quality which they might be said to hold in common. Some were very smart, some were not smart; some did lots of school work, some did very little. Some had broken homes, some didn't. Some were minorities, some weren't. Some couldn't get along with other kids, couldn't accept criticism or conform; some could. Hal Smith was a stout blond kid who got all A's, did the work, and had his life planned; he was going to enter the Coast Guard like his father and pilot those boats across the bar. He had a notebook full of *Life* magazine pictures of tremendous waves roaring up at the mouths of Oregon rivers, of small Coast Guard boats battling them. Charles Ford was a witty child of stern Lutheran parents, who did nothing right except school work, who would only catch baseballs one-handed with a right-handed glove on his left hand and who wrote cynical and satiric papers about fairytales à la *Mad* magazine. Rosie was a girl who spent all day reading books, crouched down in her desk, which she moved to a corner, and her afternoons out of school with fruit flies, upon which she made endless experiments. Ray had already given up on school work because he couldn't do none of it, add, read, or write, and wanted to spend his days cleaning up, taking roll, investigating what other kids were doing and putting up good stuff on the board. Howard was a science-mad kid from Canada whose cum folder remarked that he, while an excellent student, wouldn't participate in sports; he was the only kid in the class who played hockey in some junior league —of course the school had no hockey league to play in. Lucy and Sally were beautiful giggly girls who wanted to interact (as we say) with me all day long. After school they sat on my car, defying me to go home. Susan was an Italian girl of great social consciousness, full of clear and accurate notions about the injustice of the world. Eileen and Rosa were Catholic girls whose main concern was their mothers' wish that they attend Catholic high school, who didn't want to do it, who kept trying to keep out of trouble in order that their mothers wouldn't have some objective reason to send them there, who knew they were going there anyway (and they did) but who wanted to make sure that there could be no reason like bad grades or bad citizenship which their mothers could call upon as justification for their actions—that their mothers would just have to say in the end, I just am going to send you there because I want to, and then they, Eileen and Rosa, would win the battle. There was Robert Chow, a fat lump of a Chinese kid who wouldn't do anything at all in school, but who was later discovered by Rosie to have been raising (or growing) fresh water clams in various tanks in his house since he was seven or eight, a feat which, so said Rosie, was thought almost impossible by the experts she was always reading.

Well, there were obviously some twenty-five or so others, too—I imagine I remember more kids from that class than from any other I've had—none of them alike, all different people as to desire, need, aspiration, even though the school had decided to classify them as being all the same, i.e., immature. Perhaps the school had hoped I would figure out some lessons aimed specifically at immaturity, that I would either cure them of immaturity or, if incurable, figure some way to teach them in spite of it; or perhaps the school only hoped I'd keep them out of everyone's hair for a year. Obviously that wasn't my concern. I hadn't invented immaturity nor been consulted about it by the school and so I could ignore it except to wonder occasionally why it was that these particular kids (and by implication, I myself) were chosen to be immature. Considering my recent past, the New World and all that, I could have brooded about the gulf between something called *learning* and something called *achieving in school,* about the teacher as authority or entertainer or provider of work—about the razor's edge you must walk, between the expectation of the kids (one to which they cling firmly, even though they may despise it) about what school *is* and your own conviction that most of that is worthless at best. In fact, though, I slipped into the year, the class, as easily as a fish into water without (as I feel) much thought about it, without trying to reform the school and the world, following the kids' leads and offering mine for them to follow, feeling good about coming to work and living easily in the classroom. Everything followed *naturally,* is what I want to say; only now, in retrospect, do I want to write down something about the way we lived in and out of school with the purpose of taking a look at that razor's edge and how you may walk it if it appears during your journey that you must.

For if we are talking about what the school wants kids to do, we are talking about seventh grade spelling books with twenty words to spell and define each week for thirty-six weeks, talking about math books with per cent problems to do and interest and decimals and review of add-subtract-etc., talking about social studies with Egypt and the Renaissance and talking about science with water cycle and gravity and health-vitamin-germs-Pasteur-don't-smoke. (The school changes textbooks; in math besides the above now it is commutative and associative to define; in science DNA and ecology and don't-take-drugs; in language it is watered-down and crude linguistics. Egypt remains.) If you feel that what the school calls learning is bullshit shall you inform your students of that and forbid them to do the school work? If you feel that

58

what the school calls learning is bullshit shall you inform the kids of that and still make them do it? If you feel that what the school calls learning is bullshit ought you to pretend that you don't feel that? Pointless questions. Arrogant questions, besides; you forget that the kids really know the score, know that no matter what you, some nutty individual teacher with whom they've been saddled for no reason of their own, think about it, they've their parents and future teachers and their cum folders and the high school counselors and achievement tests and four years of high school and college and grad school and the Coast Guard to satisfy. They have lives to lead, something which is often forgotten (I had, too, a fact which became rather obtrusive around this time), and for many kids the school was only a gambit to be achieved in some way within those lives—part of them, important perhaps, but not a point of philosophy, nothing relevant, crucial only in that it shouldn't get messed up and be allowed or forced to intrude. Still, I was affected by the New World. I couldn't say that the school work was learning. I couldn't judge the students on the basis of whether they did it or not, did it well or O.K. or lousy. Still the students were waiting for me to give out the course of study in all those academic disciplines—language, social studies, science and math—so that they could deliver another year's performance according to their own lights. So that Hal could establish another leg on the way to the Coast Guard, so that Charles could satisfy his notion of what he ought to do before doing what he liked, so that Eileen and Rosa could have something to use against their mothers, so that Rosie could have something to not-do, so that Ray could have something going on to observe and approve and disapprove (he was of course the greatest judge and moralist of school work, as are most kids who get F's in school). What—should I refuse the kids this staple of their existence? Refuse them an item they had good use for? Not likely. On the other hand, was I going to indicate a serious attachment to this bullshit? Not likely either. I got in all the textbooks the school had, in all the subjects, got the supplementary books, the high, average and low readers, math puzzles, Lifes in Syrias (tangential to Egypt), Negro histories, Clouds and Bugs, Flax and Other Products, Atlases, and so on. I put up on the board segments of each to be done (read and questions answered about) each week or (in the end) each month, according to a simple schedule which would allow for the completion of this work in these books by the end of the year, supposing some kid wanted to complete this work in these books by the end of the year. I made ditto sheets of my own about form classes in the new grammar, about why Egyptians showed both feet pointing the same way, about "The Rocking Horse Winner," about why ice is lighter than water.

Only I refused to pretend that I had to "teach" any of that stuff. We all knew it was stuff to do, rather than anything which had to be learned or even could be learned. I knew that most of the kids could already do it if they wanted or needed to do it, and that some of the kids couldn't do it because they really couldn't read or figure it, which was because it was against the principles of their lives to do it. It is the old German notion of apprenticeship; this year you get a nail, the next year you get a hammer, the next you get to hit the nail with the hammer. I know that is crazy and the kids know it is crazy and the Germans know it is crazy but we also know that is how things are, even if we don't know how they got that way or who decided it. If we want to be carpenters or enter the Coast Guard we'll hold still for this craziness, knowing that it has nothing at all to do with whether or not we become good carpenters or with how we will finally encounter the breakers off the Oregon coast, for that is entirely up to us at that point in the river where everything narrows, the game narrows, and it is up to our individual courage as men, women, girls, and boys.

But look what happens when you do that. You don't have to stand up in front of the class and make everyone shut up and listen to you as you explain the assignment, demonstrate how to work equations, point out what metaphors are . . . you don't have to pretend that order and silence have to do with learning (or even with doing school work!) and you don't have to pretend that no one can produce work without your lecture, and in short you don't have to be a contemptible ass and that is good. What you can do then is to say loudly every Monday morning that You (you students) *already know* this, *already know* what the school intends to teach you this year and any other year, that the means to produce this and satisfy the school and the Coast Guard is *already in your heads*— you get to say Quit asking me if this or that is right or if this or that ought to be capitalized or if such and such is a noun or class I word—you get to repeat (as teacher) all that kind of information is already in your heads, you only have to reach in there and get it out—you get to say I'm not playing that particular school game with you, where I start explaining and you start not-paying attention (since you don't need or can't use the explanation) and talking or fucking around and then I'm supposed to say Pay Attention and you're supposed to say I am (while you're not, since it's not necessary and therefore obligatory that you don't, while obligatory to me as teacher that you pretend you are)—you get to say: "And then went down to the ship, / Set keel to breakers, forth on the godly sea, and / We set up mast and sail on that swart ship, / Bore sheep aboard her and our bodies also . . ." and so get going with the day, the week, the journey. . . .

You get to arrive at school in your car and go drink coffee and smoke and talk (if you've someone to talk to) until the bell rings and then begin another smoke and go to the bathroom and get another cup of coffee to take to class and when you arrive late the kids are settling into the day and the room, someone is taking roll and the lunch count with some shouts about who is really here even if they aren't really *here* yet, and when you come in several kids rush you with urgent requests about going to the library or to their lockers or to phone their moms or get some other kid's homework out of a third kid's locker and you can agree or forbid or stall them, saying Wait until I have a little coffee, a number of other kids are sitting around drinking their Cokes and eating doughnuts which they've just bought on their way to school . . .

But you don't have to stand in front of the class and give out some lesson and explain things which no one needs explained to a restless group who have a lot of other things on their minds and who (as soon as you finish explaining) will ask you questions about what you just clearly explained. There's time, you can say to yourself; and when the first urgent group is dealt with and given passes and gone you can talk to the next group of kids who just want to talk, about what's going on today or what their moms said or their brother did or what outrage is being served for lunch or do you want some gum? You can have all the roll slips and lunch-count slips and hall passes and library passes and the slips for ordering movies and prints and film strips and supply-order forms available in your desk for the students to fill out and order and go get and (since they understand the bureaucracy of the school at least as well as you do) you can be assured that they will keep your desk straight and order stuff on time and keep the room well supplied with three-hole lined paper and ditto paper and paper clips and staples and take inventory of the books from time to time (faking reports for losses or stolen just as well as you will) and getting the couple of kids who have spent some diligent time learning to forge your initials do all the signing on all these slips and notify the class of assemblies and dances and games and threats from the administration and clean up the room on occasion and put up the assignments on the board and check off the papers according to who has done what of the regular work and get the mop from the custodian when paint is spilled. . . .

And then sometime during the day if it looks like the time is right or you just feel like it or indeed anxiety tells you you must do it, you can get around to getting up and standing there and telling everyone to shut up and then sum up what's going on in science or remind everyone that today we decided to read everyone's stories or say I want everyone to be careful with the goddamn paint and sometimes that is just the right thing and everyone wants to be drawn together and be a group (and sometimes it's not and you can either forget it or get tough and make everyone, if that's what you really feel like, which it sometimes is) . . . but quite possibly it will be Janet instead who has dreamed up the idea of *Culture Hour,* what this class needs is some *Culture!* (I teach her the word *Kultur,* which she likes very much) standing up there, a little blond chick yelling Shut up for Culture Hour! and an uproar of laughing and griping and sitting down because everyone really knows Janet is going to *have* Culture Hour no matter what and they might as well get it over with and besides everyone really likes the grand bullshit of the idea, and Janet then reads Robert Browning or "Hiawatha" or *The Nonsense Book* or something of her own or some other kids' stories so long as they are cultured and everyone scoffs and makes uncultured remarks and has a grand time. . . .

And while teachers are complaining they haven't any *time* you see that you have all the time in the world, time to spend with Lucy and Sally telling them they got glue on their heads and threatening them about what you're going to do if they get on the hood of your car again until they are satisfied, time with Eileen and Rosa, who have discovered that if they get caught a couple of times smoking in the bathroom their mothers will react most satisfactorily, time to talk with Howard, who has discovered simultaneously a real woods out in back of the drive-in and The Byrds and is trying to make sense out of both (the woods have foxes and a skunk and a red-tailed hawk flying overhead and some kind of marvelous purple moss which the Museum of Science don't know about and who would have thought that right here in this prototype [his word] of suburban developments there would be a real woods, and here too that is just what The Byrds are singing about)—every day there are going to be kids who want to spend some time talking to you, as adult, as teacher, as whatever you are, wanting to relate their adventures and troubles and excitements and miseries and aspirations and confusions or hoping perhaps to get some clear idea of the world they live in through you. At the same time there are going to be a lot of kids in the room who don't want to talk to you at all, that day, just want to be left alone with their school work (it may happen) or eats or books or drawings or models or to talk to each other or get mad and begin fights or arguments, they can get along very well without you, it seems, and you can let them. Then you will even have time to go round to Ray or whoever else it is and teach them something that they really need to know, not only in order to get along in the school but in order to be *equal* in America—get Ray some book to read and sit down with him awhile and read it together and *teach* him, get Robert to pull himself together enough to attempt the mystery of dividing and teach *him,* go around later on to Ray and say you *can* read, now read me some. You can teach some kids something that they need and want to know, so long as you have the time, including of course showing some kids how to do the week's or month's official work if they want to do it and are having trouble with it (if they want to be official achieving seventh graders, which oddly enough many kids want to be) or talking with kids about what they might do otherwise if they don't want to be those same official seventh graders but are interested in writing or drawing or painting or making empty gallon cans of ditto fluid cave in for Science. You have time to protect some kids and get mad at others, you have time to answer over and over again questions about what kind of cigarettes you smoke and when did you start to smoke, are you married, how many kids do you have, would you let your kids smoke, let them grow long hair, do you think Robert is really smart? what would you do if your kids cut school, got an F, smoked in the bathroom, what kind of car, what was the war like, did you get in any fights, can you dance, did you like girls when you were thirteen, don't you think the

PE teacher is unfair about giving out checks. Mrs. so-and-so said this yesterday, do you agree with that? Time to talk about all that, without worry, since the official part of the school work is going on, or not going on, without your total involvement in it. Time to read your book in there too, look at the want ads in the paper if you feel like it, telling everyone to leave you alone, time to cut out of the class and go visit the shop or the art room or some other class to see what's going on, knowing everyone will get along while you're gone. . . .

Time to live there in your classroom like a human being instead of playing some idiot role which everyone knows is an idiot role, time to see that teaching (if that is your job in America) is connected with your life and with you as a human being, citizen, person, that you don't have to become something different like a Martian or an idiot for eight hours a day. Time to deal with serious concerns of the kids and time to deal with put-on concerns and time to fuck around and time to get mad either seriously or not seriously . . . but you can only live that kind of life in there if you are willing to realize that the dicta of the school are crazy but that at the same time the kid's life is connected to the school in complicated ways and you'd better offer him the chance to take any part of it he wants or has to. These dicta do not exist in themselves. *One is not Duchess one hundred yards from a carriage.* They too are part of what Dewey would call the continuum of existence. I prefer Wittgenstein's words —the stream of life.

Perhaps now I can bring up a few other things which bear upon the stream of life. Before we left Big Bar, George told us that no one had camped there since the Depression, when, he said, as many as thirty families had lived there for months at a time. He also brought over a fresh-caught three-pound steelhead as a gift. He was taking pity on me, he said. I saw you a-fishing away like that and not gittin' any so one day I just thought to go stand out on the bluff beyond my place there for a few minutes and of course I got this one right away so I brought it over so you could at least have one to eat.

A summer later, Jay and I were driving back from the desert where we'd gone to see his grandma. He was sleeping in the back, and then all of a sudden I realized he wasn't sleeping any more but in a coma and I found the hospital in Modesto at about three in the morning. A young doctor there did about a thousand things at once and very likely saved his life. The doctor thought he might have gotten some agricultural poison or eaten deadly nightshade, but then he thought that he had encephalitis, and he was taken the next day in an ambulance to San Francisco and he stayed in the hospital there for a few weeks. Tests didn't show anything and no one could figure out what kind of encephalitis or how he'd gotten it or if and in any case there wasn't much to do except see if he lived or not, while maintaining a lot of life support at the hospital. A specialist from Oakland saw him and offered my wife the opinion that if he lived, it could only be as a kind of vegetable. I made up my mind on the spot to kill the specialist later on, as soon as things got over with.

After it became clear he would live, we took him home. We spent an odd year. Jay was simply turned off, like a radio with its tubes burnt out, or one just unplugged. All he could do was breathe and swallow. Fran spent hours every day for a year, moving joints. Bending his legs, moving feet, turning neck, wrists, ankles, shoulders, moving the joints of every finger and toe up and down, all of it done with the knowledge that it hurt. We spent hours talking to Jay, telling him stories as he lay in the bath, his head supported since he couldn't hold it up, had no voluntary control of any part of his body. The thing is, it was absolutely clear to us that he heard us, in some way understood what was happening. We could see a glint in his eye, perhaps. So that when one day he could hold up his own head, when he could sit up, when he could move his own finger, when he could crawl . . . then we could be elated just like when Jack began to crawl as a

66

baby and believe even more in that glint or ghost in his eyes. Yet when Jay began to try to talk again it was the opposite of Jack learning to talk. For in Jay's head it was clear he knew what he wanted to say, but that he just didn't know how to get his mouth and tongue in shape to say it, whereas Jack could produce any sound he wanted, he just didn't have anything much to say, being only about a year old.

Well, this was going on during the time of the classes I've written about. I'm sure I have a couple of years put together in there, and I know the exact chronology is wrong in some way. Let me just add that you get an entirely different idea of societies like Easter Seal and such if you really need help from them and if you get it in the form of help with physical therapy and occupational therapy; you get a different idea of doctors if your own is a man who really concerns himself with your child and if, knowing that no miracles of modern medicine are going to do the trick, tells you that what you have there is not some different kid, but the same kid who needs you to help him and work with him, and who is going to be O.K.

After about a year, Jay was in shape to want, above all things, to play and be with other kids. He was then just able to totter around a little, holding on to walls and furniture. So we used to carry him down to the alley outside our flat where all the kids played and he'd sit in the sun and set up soldiers or play with cars with other kids and then they'd perhaps play ball and we'd watch Jay go crawling lickety-split after the ball when it got away from other kids, planning to get into the game on whatever terms, not knowing ourselves whether to laugh, cry or what. He also wanted to go back to school, since none of the other kids were around during the day, being in school themselves. The principal at the school he'd been to for kindergarten hemmed and hawed and did we think it was the best thing and he might get hurt and in the end she really refused, and we settled on Excelsior! School in the city, a special public school for orthopedically handicapped kids plus a scattering of severely retarded kids. A bus came every morning and picked Jay up with his football helmet on, which the school required in case he fell on his head, and at the school he got loaded onto a wheelchair until he was walking better and got out of the wheelchair, and he got therapy there and got on the bus to come home, and it was good that Excelsior! School existed. But then, after the first jubilant relief about this long, dusty road back, we began to see the evil of such a school, and, if I may say so, it is the very evil of all public schools. It is only that in the harsh light of a place where all the kids have some real handicap—i.e., they can't walk or talk or see or hear or hold things in their hands, as opposed to fake culture-invented handicaps like being poor or rich or black—the evil becomes clearer, more blatant. I began to hear from Jay that he was being kept in from recess in order that he finish his writing or math or something. He wasn't being allowed to paint because he didn't finish his workbook in time. When I heard that I felt like I was going to go crazy. I'd worked in school for many years, yet I couldn't believe it. I went down, Fran went down, we both went down, and talked to the teacher, talked to the principal. We wanted to tell them that Jay just couldn't write any faster—we tried to make it clear clinically to them that none of his movements were automatic but all relearned and had to be thought about, that he could not move quickly, couldn't think faster, that just picking up his pencil meant he had to think about which fingers, how to curve them, how to flex the muscles to grasp it, how to move his hand so that certain shapes came out, A's, B's, and C's, 2's and 4's, plusses and minuses. We tried to convince them that what Jay needed above all was to play, to start getting back that sixth year he'd entirely missed, to relocate all those seemingly random movements of play and fooling around and moving about and manipulating things on his own hook, to talk to other kids and horse around with them . . . we tried to tell them about how the Easter Seal therapists and the doctor wanted him to be doing large motor movements like specifically painting, spreading those big splashes of color onto paper . . . and we'd come home together or separately from these visits thinking it wasn't going to do any good at all or thinking we were crazy, me cursing and wanting to kill someone and crying and Fran cursing and wanting to kill someone and crying and in the end accusing each other of either not being tough enough or of being too tough and antagonizing the school (what if they were right? what if they take it out on Jay?) and fighting among ourselves and being insane enough to get hold of Jay when he came home and tell him for God's sake to try and work faster. . . . I shake right now with absolute rage when I remember the calm teacher and the firm principal telling us that perhaps Jay was a little lazy, after all, kids, you know . . . (and in my mind he is crawling along the alley on banged-up and scraped knees after a baseball in order to be playing) and affording us the school philosophy that handicapped kids, being handicapped, ought to be just a little bit better in everything than regular kids, having their handicaps to get over, which was just about what the black teachers used to say (perhaps still do) at the black school I taught at, you black kids got to be nicer and more disciplined and more conformist, since, having that initial handicap, you got to have an MA to get that janitor's job . . . yet that was the only school he could go to, yet they were giving him quite excellent physical therapy, yet he was going to have to get along with the school, still how can such a kid possibly be called in the name of reason anything like lazy, still he needs to play, still how can it be important about nine minus what when he had still got to stand there and figure out deliberately and consciously how to move hand and arm and doorknob so that the door opens when he wants it to?

Just so. Just so the public school practices alienation on the land, and it is a practice which affects its teachers, its kids and the parents of its kids alike, some obviously more harshly than others. You may be sure you

69

know everything about your kid, or about how you want to teach, or about yourself as a kid, but if the school tells you different you'll find that wedge driven in there between you and your child, between you and your class, between yourself as you know yourself and yourself as the school tells you about yourself.

In the end, I was able to decide to take Jay out of Excelsior! School and take him out to Tierra Firma School in my own district where I knew and admired the principal and the teachers, a small public school with big grass fields and no stairs (it always interested me that a school for orthopedically handicapped children should have three floors of stairs to climb)—but that was after Jay was walking pretty good and even able to run a little, and because being a teacher I had the opportunity to make the change. But before that I visited Excelsior! one day when Jay was in the third grade, still being kept in from recess quite a bit, and his group of kids was facing the teacher who was holding up flash cards about math, while the kids gave the answers. I sat in back of Jay. From where he sat the light came in through the window at just the right angle so that when the teacher held up the card to him the card was made semi-transparent and he could see the answer. So could I. The teacher kept holding up the cards and Jay kept reading the answer off the back, 17, 22, 11, 4, working his tongue and lips around to make sure the sound came out right. When I left, the pleased teacher told me Jay's math was really improving and I said I was happy to see it and when Jay got home he looked sidewise at me and asked if I happened by any chance to notice that you could see the answers on the backs of the cards, and I said yeah, I did just happen to notice that and then he grinned and said I sit right there every day at math time—and we have math the same time every day!

And I laughed and told Jay he was a no-good tricky wart and felt the weight of Excelsior! School fall off me and I was rid of it forever. Jay had figured out the school and gotten a break with the sun at eleven in the morning

and knew how to use it and that was when I knew un-
questionably that he was going to be O.K., and I could
stop wanting to kill someone because that evil was just a
fake too, for you might have to be there where it was
going on but you didn't have to fall for it, you didn't
have to practice it or abet it or even battle it on its
own terms, you could just tell it to go take a flying fuck
at the moon and it would be displayed as a shadow,
powerless, unless you—you parents, teachers and kids—
give it power.

The kids in my class were all stubborn, I said. Perhaps
that was why they were called immature. Not only was
Ray stubborn in refusing to do school work and also
refusing to do nothing, not only were the girls stubborn
in refusing to stop using the school to force their mothers
out into the open, not only was Rosie stubborn in refusing to stop reading her books during math lesson, but
Hal and Charles and Howard were stubborn too, in refusing to submit to the school's intention that they just do
the work and get A's. They had what they thought of as
their futures to consider and wanted to *learn* something
from that work, doing the work better than was wanted
and spending too much time on it, demanding fuller
explanations for which teachers had *no time,* messing up
the schedule of work. Still that is only my reasoning now.
At the time I occasionally wondered, Why were these kids
called immature?

It happened somewhere along all the above, in time,
that what we all were interested in was the intramural
sports program. We entered football and basketball and
got regularly smeared. But in baseball season, we developed a big hit-and-run Chicago White Sox-type team (I
was reading Bill Veeck's biography at the time). The girls
came down and led cheers, we held practice sessions and
got lucky, and near the end of the year we entered the
finals, the World Series of Spanish Main School. Winning
junior high softball teams are usually composed of two
or three big guys who hit the ball a mile, perhaps two

71

actual good ballplayers who field well and can make the right play, and the rest bums like everyone else. The effort of the team is to talk the big guys into showing up for the game at noon, instead of going off with the girls or for a smoke, and then the good ballplayers get on with well-placed singles and perhaps a bum or two gets on base off an error, and then the big guy gets up and hits the ball three miles and the team wins. We had Sam, who supposedly could hit the ball a mile but who in fact almost always struck out. For the rest we had medium-sized fair ballplayers—no one really great, but also no one really horrible. Even Charles with his wrong-handed glove usually caught the ball out in right field. We got into the finals by actually throwing out guys who hit grounders, by catching fly balls, by hitting grounders to the bums on the other team and taking second after their bums threw it over the first baseman's head, by playing what we called "heads-up" ball, by not arguing too much among ourselves, and mainly by showing up for every game so that we won quite a number by default. Well, at that time there was usually quite a crowd showing up for the Series, four out of seven games on consecutive noontimes, and while we got respect for even being there at all, no one gave us a chance. The other team had three big well-known Monsters, a couple of belligerent All Star good ballplayers, and they murdered us the first game, making no errors (therefore we didn't score) and the Monsters cleaning up for about ten runs. Two of the Monsters didn't show for the second game, and we won. We won the third too, since their two All Stars got into a fist fight about who should have handled a grounder between third and short and got thrown out of the game. After that they were afflicted with internal dissension, as the sports pages call it, and sent down their teacher to ask for a postponement the next day. We stood on our rights and refused, winning therefore by default.

The next morning Hal discussed with me a plan which, he said, he'd had in mind all year. It concerned the rules for junior high intramural softball—in this case, the particular rule against stealing bases, a rule made because the catchers were always bums and couldn't catch or throw. The rule said that the runner must keep his foot on the bag until the ball leaves the pitcher's hand. Hal thought that rule somewhat ambiguous. What if, he said, their runner is on base, and I start to pitch the ball, only instead of letting it go at the end of the swing I just hold onto it? Well, I said, that'll be a balk. Sure he said, a balk. The runner could take second base. But when the ball is supposed to leave my hand, the guy running is going to take his foot off the base to get going. When I hold on to it, there he'll be off the bag. He's gotta be out!

We talked about it. The other kids gathered around offering opinions. The issue came to be whether the guy would be out before he took second base, whether the balk or the foot off the bag took precedence. No one knew, but Hal reasoned that the kid umpire wouldn't know either. He figured either way we couldn't lose, if he pulled it at the right time, namely when they had a guy on base and their Monster up to bat. Either the guy on base would be out, leaving the Monster with nothing to clean up even if he hit a homer, or else their team would get mad during the argument over the rules and they might even have another fight, and default, or just be so mad they couldn't play well. It was worth a try.

We went out the next noontime, loading in games 3–1. About the fourth inning it was 0–0, their Monsters having only hit fly balls a mile up into the air. Then, with one out, they got a belligerent All Star on base and a Monster up to bat. Hal threw a couple way outside to the Monster. Each time he let it go, the All Star dashed halfway to second. Then Hal wound up, flung the ball viciously—and held on to it! He just stood there, holding out the ball at arm's length. The All Star stood frozen in his tracks halfway to second. The Monster stood there, bat cocked to hit the ball downtown. You could have put the whole tableau in a museum, like Raising The Flag At Iwo Jima.

Then hell broke loose. The other team rushed the poor

kid umpire, led by the furious All Star. Our team rushed the umpire. The rest of the school, our girl cheerleaders, watching teachers . . . yelling, pulling, shoving, God almighty, a perfect or awful scene, depending upon how you looked at it. In the end, the umpires didn't know what to do about it, of course, and finally the PE coach in charge of the games got the idea of what all the argument was about and said Balk! Balk! Play ball! Then Hal rushed him, the coach, and tried to talk about the ambiguity of the rule and how could it be just a balk since it had to be an out too? and by that time I'd rushed the coach too, remembering that was what we managers were supposed to do, but he just told me and Hal to get the hell out of there. Hal, however, couldn't let it go at that. He had to explain to the coach how he'd figured out about the rule and that the coach couldn't just say Balk! not logically anyway, and that was when the coach got the idea for the first time that it was a deliberate thing, that Hal had planned it all, just to fuck up the game and cause trouble, just to get any kind of advantage, and so he told us to shut up and start playing ball or forfeit the game.

He was really angry, and after the game (which we lost about 10–0 again, losing the next two by similar scores also) he came over and said What you guys pulled today was the most *immature* thing I ever saw! He was a guy I liked and respected at the school, by the way, and he meant that if you find some chink in the armor of the school or the game you ought to let it alone and just take your lumps. Still, Hal and all of us didn't figure to take our lumps if we didn't have to, and we also thought along with Bill Veeck that if we did, someone was going to have to take theirs too. So despite my present speculations, it was right then that I learned why it was that the school had pegged us all as immature, and I know it was something worth learning.

Part Two

Explanatory Notes

Explanatory Note #1

FIND A GOOD SCHOOL AND SEND YOUR KID THERE

If Excelsior! School deals with really disadvantaged kids then Tierra Firma Elementary deals with advantage. Its kids come from Tierra Firma itself, the first suburb of San Francisco, discovered or invented for the reason all suburbs are discovered or invented—its people hope to drop out of the problems of America and enjoy its promise.

The people of Tierra Firma are the advantaged of America. They make enough money to afford cheap developer-built houses, cars, boats, bowling balls and plenty of Sta-Prest pants, but, since that is true of many other groups of people in America, including the rich, that is not the source of their advantage. They are advantaged because they believe in the promise of America and are actually satisfied by it when they get it and by the striving which they must constantly do to keep getting and believing in it. They believe, for instance, that as long as you are free to buy things on credit then you can keep going to work in order to pay those payments and that the one justifies the other and makes it meaningful. They know what you are supposed to do and by and large make an effort to do it and see the results and they are not cynical about the results. They have perhaps moved from big old Mission Street or North Beach wooden carpenter-Gothic houses and flats, where the plumbing is always going out of whack and streetcars run past the door, to three-bedroom tract houses with a back yard and a palm tree in the front and a garage and streets where the kids can ride bikes, and they are glad they did so. Middle-class and rich people disdain Tierra Firma and move into those same old wooden houses and pay $40,000 and another $20,000 to fix them up good because they are not satisfied with America, just like the poor who have to stay in them without fixing them up. The advantaged move to Tierra Firma. They are advantaged because, I repeat, America still holds promise for them; if you do right, you can really get all this that Tierra Firma affords, and since that is exactly what they do want, and since they can get it, they are satisfied. No doubt many of them understand the political and economic manipulations necessary in order for Tierra Firma to exist; no doubt they have gripes about property tax and this and that; no doubt they know the poor exist and something perhaps ought to be done about it; no doubt many are against the war; no doubt they are not all racists; and no doubt they know the TV ads are phony . . . but they are cast in the present right image of the country and know that they can and will make it in America *because they are really satisfied* with what they have got out of it. I know that if you hang around with liberal intellectuals or with militant Third World people or with poor people or with radical college students or, simply, if you hang around with people who are dissatisfied with the state of affairs, you will get the idea, and hope it is true, that most people in America are dissatisfied and then you will predict major changes in the country. To correct that mistaken state of mind, I hope you will go to work in Tierra Firma someday.

The fact remains that Tierra Firma Elementary School is one of the best public schools I have ever seen, and that is why I took Jay out there to school, and why, when Jack decided he'd like to go out there too, I took both my boys. It is a good school because of the principal, and because of the teachers whom he collected together over the rather long period of time that he has been principal there. It is a good school because for a few years there was a district superintendent who tried to get intelligent, serious people to come to work in the district and, once they did, allowed them to work. I have a good deal of respect for all the people involved in Tierra Firma School; they are, by and large, exactly the kinds of people that educational writers are always saying ought to be working with kids in schools. They are bright, serious, hardworking, confident, innovative, humorous, well-read, creative, with-it. They are not repressive, narrow, grade-oriented, vain, afraid, hung-up on testing, conventional, or chickenshit. They have guts; they like and respect the kids. The school itself is O.K. In modern one-story motel style, all the rooms open directly to the outdoors. There is plenty of space—a large asphalt play area for basketball, bikes and four-square, a big grass area, a little-kids' playground with swings and slides and monkey bars and tanbark, and a huge upper field of grass which is what convinced Jay to go there. He could see himself running free on that big grass field, looking like a whooping crane about to take off.

All right. But see, this is the same school that Fran visited and all the kids were running around on that really pleasant playground yelling about murder and MR and fuck you. That is what the kids are supposed to be doing in them no-good schools, in them ghetto schools, in them big-city pore schools, in them rich hippie dope-smoking schools, in them terrible repressive tracked grade-mad bureaucratic lesson-planned honky colonialist Fascist pig Cossack San Francisco schools with Irish or Italian old ladies who ought to have been nuns or ex-Navy disappointed commanders for principals. That is not what, in theory and on principle, kids are supposed to be doing in what few good schools there are in existence, for in fact the very reason for making the effort to have any good schools is so that the kids won't be in this bad shape. So why, if it's really a good school ain't it doing any good? Why is it that in this good school with these good people that Jack, in the first grade, who is really what everyone agrees is an excellent student—he can read, as far as I can see, anything, he can write, and not only that but he likes to draw and write and read a good deal of the time, he can in short do everything that the school, any school, wants him to be able to do and not only that but he is wise enough to be reasonably well behaved and polite when it counts . . . why is it that if one day on the way to this good school he realizes that in his urgency to get up to Mr. Ling's corner store and buy some fake wax teeth to show off and later chew, he has forgotten to bring along his homework in writing or math . . . why is it that then he bursts into tears? Why is it that then no effort of mine will console him? Why is he frightened? He, of all kids going to that good school, has the least reason to be frightened.

There is one reason, and only one, and it is crucial. That is that an American public school must have winners and losers. It does not matter in this respect what kind of school it is. In Berkeley, now that Mr. Sullivan has integrated the schools, it is the black kids who sit in Remedial Reading and the white kids who sit in Enriched this or that. When they are together in some general course the well-dressed sharp clean-and-pressed shoe-shined pore black kid sits in class next to the Salvation-army-surplus-store-ugly-dressed white rich kid and the beautiful pore black kid doesn't know what the teacher is talking about and the white ugly rich kid knows everything and can read or even has read everything the teacher can, even if that surplus-store white kid disdains the whole thing and won't answer or discuss or even attend class, even if he goes and smokes shit across the street or heads for the communal hills . . . try as he may to become an outcast the school knows that he is a winner even if he rejects winning. The intelligent hip young teacher will be copying his ugly clothes while pretending to try and straighten him out, get him off drugs, interest him in Egypt, which the teacher probably don't know nothing about. Or the intelligent old conservative teacher will be talking in the teachers' room about how bright the long-haired ugly-clothes kid is even if a pain in the ass and that the school must find a way to motivate him, or force him, the country needs him, and so on. After class the black kid finds eight other black kids who have just had the same classroom experience and they link arms and walk jiving down the hall, covering the passageway wall to wall, forcing every one of them ugly know-it-all white play-poor winning motherfuckers with professor-fathers to change direction, go around the other way, shrink up against the wall. This phenomenon is then called racial unrest.

But over in Oakland there will be an all-black school, Mr. Sullivan not having passed through that town yet. It may be that the school would prefer to have some ugly white kids to be winners, but they in fact ain't got any. Does that mean a school full of losers? Not at all. That school has got to have winners too, and so some sharp pore beautiful black kids wind up in the A group and some others in the H group. It may be that if the kids in the Oakland A winner's group transferred over to Berkeley they would end up being losing kids, or it may be not. It doesn't make any difference. In Oakland they are winners. The H kids find the A kids in line at the cafeteria and hit them in they mouths.

In Tierra Firma, up until recently, all the kids have been these same advantaged lower-middle-class kids (white, black and brown) I've already mentioned. They ain't by and large ugly rich Army-Navy-store whites nor lime-green-creased pore beautiful blacks. So therefore the school only has winners? Certainly not. What kind of school would that be? Some of them advantaged kids have got to lose. It may be that if the losers of Tierra Firma transferred to Berkeley or Oakland then they would be winners. Or it may not be. The students who end up in a place like M.I.T. are certainly the winners of the Western world, the smartest, most with-it, craftiest Western technological human beings ever produced but even then all of them cannot be winners. Some of them must flunk out, because M.I.T. being a school in America has also

81

got to have losers. Would those M.I.T. losers be winners at S.F. State? Maybe so and maybe not.

That is why Jack, my beloved son of seven years, bursts into tears and cannot be consoled. That is why some students of M.I.T. are throwing dodge balls at each other's heads, and a large group of physicists stands around the outskirts of the school grounds crying, and why nothing can console them even if someone hits them or doesn't hit them in they mouths.

They cry because the losers are going to get some revenge some way. But they also cry because the winning is never permanent. You may be a winner in the first grade, but by the fourth you may be losing. The rites of passage of the school go on and on. Each year it is circumcision time all over again; obviously you may weep for what has been hacked off by the time you are thirty-five and have a PhD.

How does the school make certain that it will have winners and losers? Well, obviously by giving grades. If you give A's, you must also give F's. Without the rest of the grades, the A is meaningless. Even a B is less good than an A—in short, every kid who does not get an A is failing and losing to some extent. The median on the bell curve is not a median, it is not an average, it is not a norm, not to the school and not to the kids in the school. It is a losing sign, a failure, and a hex. You must be way out there on the right-hand edge where the curve approaches the base line. But it is the nature of bell curves that most everyone cannot be there.

But even if the school abandons grades and IQ and achievement testing it will still produce losers aplenty and winners. The fundamental act of the American public school is to deal with children in groups. Once it has a group of children of any age, it decides what those children will be expected to do, and then the teacher, as representative of the school, tells the children all at once. The children hear it, and when they hear it they know whether they can do it or not. Some of the children will already know how to do it. They will win. The teacher comes into the teachers' room the first day and says I already know who the good students are. I can predict the grades of almost every kid. Sure enough, the prediction works with minimum variation.

You deal with the children in groups. You teach first graders to read. You write *ch* on the board, and ask Who knows how this sounds? Some kids already know and raise their hands with tremendous relief. They are going to make it this year. Others think they know, but aren't sure. (Maybe *ch* has changed since their mamas told them.) Others never heard of it. They might be happy to know what it sounds like (why not?) but at the same time they see that a lot of other smart kids already know.

Whatever class, age group, grade, section it is, in a public school, the subject matter is carefully arranged so that some of the kids will already know it before they get there. Then, for a little while in the primary grades, the school will try to teach those who didn't know it already. But it doesn't really work. It doesn't work because the winners keep intruding, raising their hands in advance of the question, or because while the teacher works with the losers on what the winners already know the winners are free to read or draw or talk to one another and therefore learn other stuff and when the loser gets into the second grade, having learned what the school demanded that he knew before he entered the first grade, the second grade will have assessed what the winners know and the losers don't and produce that as the subject matter for the year. Later on, of course, the school will refuse to teach the losers at all. *In all public schools in the United States* the percentage of kids who cannot really read the social studies textbook or the science textbook or the directions in the New Math book or the explanations in the transformational grammar book is extraordinarily high. Half the kids. The school tells everyone that reading is the key to success in school, and no doubt it is, a certain kind of reading anyway. Does the school then spend time and effort teaching those kids who can't read the texts how to read the texts? Shit no, man. Why mess up a situation made to order for failure? At Spanish Main Intermediate School there are some eleven hundred students, at least half of whom can't read the books they lose and have to pay money for at the end of the year. The school hires one remedial reading teacher, who will only deal with about forty students per year. Even then, this teacher will not really teach the kids to read, but of course will review some complicated and nutty system which (again) some of the remedial reading students already know (although they can't read) and the others don't, for the remedial reading class is part of the school too. Well of course the school says it ain't got money enough for all them remedial reading teachers, otherwise it would love to teach everyone to read. But it does have money enough for a million social studies teachers to teach Egypt to groups of kids, a small percentage of whom already know everything about it, a large percentage of whom know enough to copy the encyclopedia, the text, or other kids' homework, and another large percentage of whom can't do anything but sit there, get in trouble, provide jobs for counselors and disciplinary vice-principals and consultants and psychologists (all of whom get paid to deal with problems the school causes every day) and become an unending supply of failure for the school.

So Jack does not misinterpret the school. Were you thinking that the homework was given to see if he could do it? To see if he had learned what was taught? You haven't learned your lesson. The homework was given to the winners to see if they would do it that night and bring it the next day. (It was given to the losers to show them they couldn't do it.) If they forget or refuse, they may have to stop being winners. For the fate of winners in a school is that they must do, over and over again, exercises and reviews and practices and assignments that they already know how to do, over and over again for twelve years, then four more, then four more . . . just as Jack has got to stop reading his books every morning in order to get ready to go to school in order to spend time doing workbooks and exercises so that he'll learn to read his books.

The school's purpose is not teaching. The school's purpose is to separate sheep from goats. You can find a very good school with lots of grass where the teachers don't yell at you. It separates. By all means send your kid there.

Explanatory Note #2

JAIL

Of course I have forgotten to tell you again, what you already know. That is that the fundament of the school, even before winners and losers, is that everyone has got to go there.

Even if you are rich or have eccentric or far-out parents and go to private schools or invent free schools for yourself, you still deal with the public school. But in any case most of you are not or have not any of the above. You must go to school.

If kids in America do not go to school, they can be put in jail. If they are tardy a certain number of times, they may go to jail. If they cut enough, they go to jail. If their parents do not see that they go to school, the parents may be judged unfit and the kids go to jail.

You go to jail. All of the talk about *motivation* or *inspiring* kids to learn or *innovative* courses which are *relevant* is horseshit. It is horseshit because there is no way to know if students really are interested or not. No matter how bad the school is, it is better than jail. Everyone knows that, and the school knows it especially. A teacher comes into the teachers' room and says happily, I had the greatest lesson today! and goes on to tell the other envious teachers what it was that they hadn't thought of themselves and says, The kids were all so excited! It is horseshit. The teacher has forgotten (as I forget) that the kids have to be there or they will go to jail. Perhaps the grand lesson was merely more tolerable

86

than the usual lesson. Perhaps the kids would have rejected both lessons if they could.

That is why the school cannot ever learn anything about its students. Why famous psychologists can successfully threaten pigeons into batting ping-pong balls with their wings, but can never learn anything about pigeons.

As long as you can threaten people, you can't tell whether or not they really want to do what you are proposing that they do. You can't tell if they are inspired by it, you can't tell if they learn anything from it, you can't tell if they would keep on doing it if you weren't threatening them.

You cannot tell. You cannot tell if the kids want to come to your class or not. You can't tell if they are motivated or not. You can't tell if they learn anything or not. All you can tell is, they'd rather come to your class than go to jail.

Explanatory Note #3

NO MAN

I have heard a teacher come into the teachers' room at report-card time and, after making out grades on those slips of paper, lean back and sigh and then say, for everyone to hear, Just look! Three-fourths of the students in my class have gotten D's!

The teacher received a gratifying murmur of sympathy from the rest of the room. We've all had them classes, they seemed to say. What a job this is! No one offered to mention how it was that those kids all got those D's. The teacher showed no sign at all of remembering that the kids in her class got those D's precisely because she had just taken her pen and written the letter D on three-fourths of the report cards.

That is the only reason they got D's. That is the only reason they became a group of D-getting kids whose teacher ought to be given sympathy. If she had written down A's instead, they would have been a group whose teacher deserved congratulations and envy. Either way, it would still be the teacher who took a pen and wrote down the D or the A on the card. The card then magically became the kid. The cards then magically became the group. I repeat, the teacher took a pen and wrote down D. Someone, a person, did it. Took the pen and wrote down D and . . .

The teacher genuinely does not realize that the class has D's only because the teacher herself just wrote down D's with her own hand, her own pen, in her free period, on slips of paper which are prepared to receive any mark at all. All she remembers is that *this class got D's,* the dumb, recalcitrant sons of bitches.

A study was done once on teacher dreams. These dreams were full of anxiety, and things kept happening which no one could account for. The teacher couldn't find her room, or he couldn't find his roll book, or the kids wouldn't sit down, and the principal and the consultant and the superintendent came in and all of a sudden the teacher had forgotten to wear any pants or she was naked and the administrators were frowning . . . what the study didn't mention was that those are the same dreams students have. I've had dreams in which I was trying to find my high school biology class and I wandered through unfamiliar halls which ought to have been familiar, trying to figure out what I had been doing the whole year and wondering what I was going to say to the biology teacher who was giving (I knew) the final test today and I didn't know anything about it and somewhere along the way of that dream I would change into being the teacher and the students were the ones who knew all about it and I didn't know what questions to ask in this final test and my pants had been stolen and how in the world could I have a hard-on right now sticking up above the desk even if I tried to stoop down, and there was the goddamn principal, all dressed up, waiting.

Well, these are classic dreams. They occur to people who do not imagine that it is they themselves who determine what happens wherever it is they work. Teachers imagine that they determine nothing. After all, who built the school? Not the teachers. Who decided that there would be thirty-eight desks in each room? Not the teachers. Who decided that thirty-eight kids in Room 3 ought to learn about Egypt in the seventh grade from 10:05 to 10:50? Not the teachers. Who decided that there ought to be forty-five minutes for lunch and that there ought to be stewed tomatoes in those plastic containers? Not the teachers. Who decided about the curriculum and who decided about the textbooks? Not us. Not us! All we know is that we have this room and thirty-eight kids come in and if there are thirty-eight desks it's perfectly clear that the thirty-eight kids belong in the thirty-eight desks and therefore ought to sit down in them, and if we have thirty-eight books of one sort or another it's obvious that each of the thirty-eight kids ought to get one, and now that they have one it's also logical that we ought to assign something to read and do in them, and in order to do that we have to talk and if some kids talk while we talk we get to explain the logic of the situation to them at length just as I have done here, and then having assigned something it's apparent that we ought to collect the assignments and it's reasonable to give some kids A and some F . . . but in the end it ain't our fault. We had nothing to do with it. It ain't our fault!

We feel we have nothing to do with it, beyond the process of managing what is presented to us. Presented to us by whom? The principal? But the principal tells us at faculty meetings that this is the situation, he didn't invent it, we all must only live with it. The superintendent? He gives us an inspiring speech on opening day, but beyond that he makes it clear that our problems are not his invention. We are all in the same boat, he wants to tell us. The board of education? The state board? The superintendent of public instruction? No, man, they didn't do it. Who decided that Egypt is just right for seventh graders? Who decided that DNA must be something which all kids answer questions about? Who decided that California Indians must enter the world of fourth grade kids, or that South America must be "learned" by sixth graders?

Nobody, it seems, made any of these decisions. Noman did it. Noman is responsible for them. The people responsible for the decisions about how schools ought to go are dead. Very few people are able to ask questions of dead men. So we treat those decisions precisely as if dead men made them, as if none of them are up to us live people to make, and therefore we determine that we are not responsible for any of them. It ain't our fault! It ain't our fault!

That is exactly what the kids say. Accepting that, it follows that we must also accept classic dreams.

Explanatory Note #4

THE DUMB CLASS

One afternoon during our free seventh period
someone looked around and said This faculty is
the Dumb Class.

It was so. Given the community or the entire country
as a school—reversing the usual image of the school as
mirror of society to make society the mirror of the school
—and given that community as one which is tracked or
ability-grouped into high, high-average, average, low-average, high-low, low and low-low, the faculty or faculties,
teachers, *educators,* are the dumb class.

We are the dumb class because we cannot learn. Cannot achieve. Why not? Cannot concentrate, have a low
attention span, are culturally deprived, brain-damaged,
non-verbal, unmotivated, lack skills, are anxiety-ridden,
have broken homes, can't risk failure, no study habits,
won't try, are lazy . . . ? Those are the reasons *kids* are
in the dumb class, supposing we don't say it's because they
are just dumb. But the characteristic of the dumb class
is that it cannot learn how to do what it is there to do.
Try as one may, one cannot make the dumb class learn
to do these things, at least not as long as it is operating
together as a dumb class. Even if those things are completely obvious, the dumb class cannot learn them or
achieve them.

Is it so that what the dumb class is supposed to achieve
is so difficult that only superior individuals can achieve it,
and then only with hard work, endless practice? Is it so
mysterious and opaque that only those with intelligence

92

and energy enough to research and ferret out the mysteries of the universe can gain insight into it? Eighth period I was involved with this dumb class which was supposed to achieve adding and subtracting before it got out of the eighth grade and went to high school. Could the class achieve it? No sir. Given an adding problem to add, most of the dumb class couldn't add it. Those who did add it hadn't any notion of whether or not they'd added it correctly, even if they had. They asked me Is this right? Is this right? This ain't right, is it? What's the answer? If you don't know whether it's right or not, I'd say, then you aren't adding it. Is this right? screamed four kids, rushing me waving papers. Boy, this dumb class can't learn, I'd say to myself. Not a very sophisticated remark, perhaps.

For a while I would drop in on the Tierra Firma bowling alley, since Jay and Jack were always dying to go there. One day I ran into the dumbest kid in the dumb class. Rather, he came up to us as we were playing this baseball slot machine. Jay and Jack were not defeating the machine, to say the least, and as a result had to put in another dime each time they wanted to play again. Well the dumb kid showed us how to lift the front legs of the machine in just the right way so that the machine would run up a big score without tilting, enough for ten or so free games, all by itself. After it did that, he told us, you could go ahead and really play it for fun. Jay and Jack were pretty impressed; they thought this dumb kid was a genius. Those big kids in your school sure are smart, was how Jack put it.

Well, as Jay and Jack happily set out to strike out and pop-up to the infield on the machine for those free games, the dumb kid and I walked around and watched the bowlers and had a smoke and talked. In the end, of course, I asked him what he was doing around there. He was getting ready to go to work, he told me. Fooling around until five, when he started. What did he do? I keep score, he told me. For the leagues. He kept score for two teams at once. He made fifteen bucks for a couple

93

of hours. He thought it was a great job, making fifteen bucks for something he liked to do anyway, perhaps would have done for nothing, just to be able to do it.

He was keeping score. Two teams, four people on each, eight bowling scores at once. Adding quickly, not making any mistakes (for no one was going to put up with errors), following the rather complicated process of scoring in the game of bowling. Get a spare, score ten plus whatever you get on the next ball, score a strike, then ten plus whatever you get on the next two balls; imagine the man gets three strikes in a row and two spares and you are the scorer, plus you are dealing with seven other guys all striking or sparing or neither one . . . The bowling league is not a welfare organization nor part of Headstart or anything like that and wasn't interested in giving some dumb kid a chance to improve himself by fucking up their bowling scores. No, they were giving this smart kid who had proved to be fast and accurate fifteen dollars because they could use a good scorer.

I figured I had this particular dumb kid now. Back in eighth period I lectured him on how smart he was to be a league scorer in bowling. I pried admissions from the other boys, about how they had paper routes and made change. I made the girls confess that when they went to buy stuff they didn't have any difficulty deciding if those shoes cost $10.95 or whether it meant $109.50 or whether it meant $1.09 or how much change they'd get back from a twenty. Naturally I then handed out bowling-score problems and paper-route change-making problems and buying-shoes problems, and naturally everyone could choose which ones they wanted to solve, and naturally the result was that all the dumb kids immediately rushed me yelling Is this right? I don't know how to do it! What's the answer? This ain't right, is it? and What's my grade? The girls who bought shoes for $10.95 with a $20 bill came up with $400.15 for change and wanted to know if that was right? The brilliant league scorer couldn't decide whether two strikes and a third frame of eight amounted to eighteen or twenty-eight or whether it was one hundred eight and one half.

The reason they can't learn is because they are the dumb class. No other reason. Is adding difficult? No. It is the dumb class which is difficult. Are the teachers a dumb class? Well, we are supposed to teach kids to "read, write, cipher and sing," according to an old phrase. Can we do it? Mostly not. Is it difficult? Not at all. We can't do it because we are a dumb class, which by definition can't do it, whatever it is.

Yet what we are supposed to do is something which, like adding, everyone knows how to do. It isn't mysterious, nor dependent on a vast and intricate knowledge of pedagogy or technology or psychological tests or rats. Is there any man or woman on earth who knows how to read who doesn't feel quite capable of teaching his own child or children to read? Doesn't every father feel confident that his boy will come into the bathroom every morning to stand around and watch while the father shaves and play number games with the father and learn about numbers and shaving at the same time? Every person not in the dumb class feels that these things are simple. Want to know about Egypt? Mother or father or older brother or uncle or someone and the kid go down to the public library and get out a book on Egypt and the kid reads it and perhaps the uncle reads it too, and while they are shaving they may talk about Egypt. But the dumb class of teachers and public educators feel that these things are very difficult, and they must keep hiring experts and devising strategies in order that they can rush these experts and strategies with their papers asking Is this right? and What's my grade?

Yet, released from the dumb class to their private lives, teachers are marvelous gardeners, they work on ocean liners as engineers, they act in plays, win bets, go to art movies, build their own houses, they are opera fans, expert fishermen, champion skeet shooters, grand golfers, organ players, oratorio singers, hunters, mechanics . . . all just as if they were smart people. Of course it is more difficult to build a house or sing Bach than it is to teach kids to read. Of course if they operated in their lives outside of the dumb class the same way they do in it, their houses would fall down, their ships would sink, their flowers die, their cars blow up.

This very morning in the San Francisco *Chronicle* I read a scandalous report. The reporter reports the revelations of a member of the board of education, namely that 45 per cent of the *Spanish-surname children* (that is how we put it in the paper these days) who are in mentally retarded classes have been found, when retested in Spanish, to be of average or above-average intelligence. The board member thought that "the Spanish-speaking kids were shunted into classes for the mentally retarded because they did not understand English well enough to pass the examinations they were given." He figured that, just like if he was told that a bowler had a spare on the first frame and got eight on his next ball, he'd figure that the bowler's score in the first frame ought to be eighteen. Well, in this matter assume that the board member is the teacher in a dumb class. He's trying to tell the school administrators something obvious. Does the administrator learn, now he's been told it, that ten and eight are eighteen? No, the assistant superintendent for special services says that "the assumption was that they understood English well enough to be tested by the English versions of the Stanford-Binet and the WISC intelligence tests." He thought that "it wasn't so much the fault of the test as it was the cultural deprivation of the child at the time of testing" which caused these smart kids to be retarded. Asked if these smart retarded Spanish-surname kids were now going to be moved into the regular program, he *revealed* that no, that wasn't the case, for they were *"still working* with the elementary division to seek a proper *transitional* program, since these children were still *functional retardates"* no matter what their IQ.

The reporter, acting in his role as critical parent, found out that the tests *were* available in Spanish but that Spanish-speaking kids *weren't* tested, therefore, in Spanish (because of the above assumption). The tests *weren't* available in "Oriental," and the "Oriental" kids *weren't* tested, therefore, in "Oriental." Well, that made sense, so the reporter pried out the information that the school district got $550 extra a year for each kid in mentally retarded classes. The reporter implied cynically that they were doing it for the money and that if they let all these bright retarded Spanish kids out there might be a shortage of $550 kids to be retarded.

But it is the dumb class we are concerned with. Here this administrator is told something obvious, told to learn it, told to achieve this difficult knowledge that them Spanish-speaking kids are only dumb if they are tested in a language they don't understand. But being in the dumb class, he don't learn it. He may be the smartest man in the world, able to keep score for league bowling, read The Book of the Dead, go water skiing, make bell curves. But in the dumb class he can't learn anything, and there is no reason to expect that he ever will as long as he is in there.

FOUR- OR FIVE-MINUTE SPEECH
FOR A SYMPOSIUM ON
AMERICAN INSTITUTIONS AND DO
THEY NEED CHANGING OR WHAT?

It's perfectly possible (I'll begin) to make remarks about institutions, for everyone is certain
to believe in the real existence of something this word
stands for—i.e., a something which exists in order to
make certain that some kind of human activity, chosen
just on account of the naturalness and inevitability of that
activity, remains natural and inevitable.

If a school is an institution, then the prerequisite inevitable activity is the natural desire of human adults to
instruct their children. They desire to instruct them in
what their world knows of magic or skill and they instruct them in the everyday ways of their world—what to
eat and how to eat it, whom you can marry, when you
may grow up, whom to obey, how to become President.

One ought then (I'll go on) to point out that institutions have characteristics, of which two seem crucial, at
least to this speech.

The first characteristic of any institution is that no matter what the inevitable purpose for which it was invented,
it must devote all its energy to doing the exact opposite.
Thus, a Savings Bank must encourage the people to borrow
money at Interest, and a School must inspire its students
toward Stupidity.

The second characteristic is that an institution must

98

continue to exist. Every action must be undertaken with respect to eternity. This second characteristic is the reason for the first. For unless a Savings Bank can persuade the people not to Save, the Savings Bank will go broke. But the Savings Bank must continue to exist, since otherwise the people would have No Place To Save. Just so, the School must encourage its students not to learn. For if the students learned quickly, most of them could soon leave the school, having Learned. But if the students left the school it would cease to exist as an institution and then the students would have No Place In Which To Learn.

Following that argument, we can arrive at a description of an institution; An Institution Is A Place To Do Things Where Those Things Will Not Be Done.

If the institutions are reproached forcefully enough, they will admit it. Thus the Savings Bank will say, You want to Save? So hide your bread under the mattress! Bury it in the back yard, you bastard!

And the School: You want to Learn? Hire a tutor! Watch TV! Get your parents to teach you! Fuck you!

An institution and its arguments are both circular. Change it? Better change the music of the spheres instead!

Change! An institution is like an English middle-class audience going to see a play by George Bernard Shaw.

Change! An institution loves change and criticism. It adapts. It endures. It is hip to the warp and woof of the nation. It perns in the gyres, if necessary. For example, if the parents of America, realizing that their child has already learned all he needs from the school, namely how to write his name, read C-A-T and recite the Preamble, wish to send him out to be apprenticed or to a job in the garment district where the child can learn about the ways of the world and at the same time make a little bread for the family, the school incites the Institution of Congress to respond with a law about Universal Education, to wit, every parent must send his child to the School until age x. (Fuck you, says the school.) A hundred

99

years later when things have changed—the kids want to work, the Union don't want them children, the nation would rather the kid went to Junior College—the school pretends that the Law was made to *make the children* go to school until age x.

Change! An old conservative general once rose to complain that the Youth had lost all respect for its Elders, that it had lost interest in the Games, that it had no Character. He did not think it would do well at another Thermopylae. He thought it had to do with the Schools. The Schools, he said, rob Youth of its Imagination, which is the only important Quality it has! In saying that, he implied that imagination and character were somehow associated, an idea which we find ludicrous.

Change! An institution can only be changed in the same way that a mountain is changed by highway engineers into a pile of dust. No institution, once invented, has ever ceased to exist. Nor has any institution ever changed, except according to the exigencies of time as above. Not changed, only adapted. Its fundamental purpose remains, namely to provide a place to do things where these things won't be done.

The School is not going to change. Criticism feeds its existence by giving it something to do, namely adapt. The school can eagerly join in criticism of its textbooks, for example, knowing that textbook publishers are preparing a billion Standard Anti-Textbooks which will show up in every class or Anti-Class some fall morning along with a neat mountain of justifying Anti-Pedagogy. The Anti-Texts will prevent learning just as well as the texts did, since they are to be used in the School. A large organized group of Anti-Parents will demand the texts back. Black Anti-Texts will have to appear. On the basis of the Anti-Texts, School administrators will get to spend their time making policy statements, getting hired, transferred and fired, and answering the telephone, proving that they still exist. . . .

So it is that institutions don't change, but people do. There is no law any more that people must go to church or pay attention to the church, and so many people don't, while others do. That is the best you can expect, and good enough. You can apparently get one institution to combat another, and it would be most useful to get rid of the law that all kids have to go to some school or other until age x or any other age. The public school is the closest thing we have in America to a national established church, Getting-An-Education the closest thing to God, and it should be possible to treat it and deal with it as the church has been treated and dealt with. This treatment has not really changed the existence of the one institution and will not harm the other, but it has allowed the growth of alternatives to it and that is what is wanted, even if some of those alternatives have become, and will become, institutions themselves.

One day I had to talk with the father of a kid in my class. The boy had been in constant trouble in school since the beginning. He would not do school work, and he refused the only alternative offered by the school, namely to do nothing. He was a bright, busy, active boy, and none of his actions fit what his teachers and the school wanted him to do, even though many of them (not all, by any means) were perfectly reasonable and even constructive in themselves. The father opened up very fiercely by informing me that he knew the boy needed discipline, that he was willing to do his part, followed with a list of punishments he was prepared to inflict and said I had his permission to be tough, to belt the kid around when he needed it, and so on. He was accepting a role which is pretty familiar to teachers—it is what they mean when they write *Parents Cooperative* on cumulative folders—that of the parent who accepts the verdict of the school about his own child.

I told him that those punishments and that insight about needing discipline weren't anything new, were they? Hadn't he and the boy's teachers agreed every year, and hadn't they belted him and restricted him and kept him after school and isolated him in the classroom and forbade TV and made him sit two hours in his room each

101

night to study and sent him to the office and paddled him and suspended him for seven years of schooldays and wasn't it clear that however wonderful and cooperative those plans were, that they hadn't worked?

Yes. He recalled that in kindergarten the boy spent an entire half year just sitting in the office, never being allowed to go to class or out to recess, because he was so bad. Then he said harshly, How can a kid that young be that bad? and (sitting there in a windbreaker and Levi's, having taken off from work to come up to cooperate with the school) burst into tears. It was a great relief to both of us. After a bit we were able to talk about our own schooldays and how we didn't always dig them nor the school us, and that we guessed we were both making it O.K. as adults no matter what the school might have thought of us, and then he said that he really thought the kid was a pretty good kid if a little wild and stubborn maybe, and how he even thought him a pretty smart kid and how good they got along together working or going out somewhere whenever he wasn't busy cooperating by not letting themselves go out or work together and by believing his boy to be stupid and bad.

He had believed that it was his duty as a parent to treat his own boy as if he didn't like him, even though he knew he did like him, because the Institution of the School knew what you were supposed to like and what you weren't, and didn't mind saying so.

That is what is meant by alternatives—namely, that none is offered the ordinary parent or the kid in America who wants to remain somehow connected to the mainstream of American life, be responsible, be a citizen, not drop or bug out of it, but doesn't want to do so or can't do so at the expense of denying what he knows of himself. There was no way I could give one to either the boy or the father, but after our talk he began to accept a kind of alternative of the mind. If the boy got in minor trouble and had to stay after school or got bad grades, the father began to ignore it, and if he was called in by teachers to cooperate he didn't come and if the boy was

102

suspended so that the father had to come to school in order to get the boy back in it (and if he didn't the boy could be sent to Juvi for truancy, remember), he began to tell them that the teachers didn't give the boy respect, they treated him badly, the vice-principal had it in for him. He always got around to asking them the same question— Why was it that a kindergarten kid ought to be kept in the office by himself all day long for half a year and how could a kid that little be so bad? It was a question that even the school was unable to answer and so the father was able to escape.

Explanatory Note #6

AT RANDOM

Some Indians, way up North, depended a lot on hunting elk for their livelihood. As long as they pursued elk along their regular hunting trails and found and killed elk, everything was O.K. But it happened every once in a while that the regular hunting trails failed to produce any elk at all. Instead of keeping on with their regular paths and starving, the Indians used magic to find the elk. The magic always worked. So some anthropologists went up to the Indians to find out what was what with that magic. Did magic work, they planned to discover, or was there some rational explanation, or was it just luck? The anthropologists sat around and watched the hunting and saw that there came a time when the elk ran out. When that happened the Indians took some elk bones out of a bag and cast them on the ground, and whichever way those bones pointed, they took off in that direction to hunt elk, and when they did that they came back with elk which they had found and killed. The magic worked. The bones were right. The anthropologists thought about it and finally realized that what was happening was that the elk, after being hunted along regular elk paths for some time, began to avoid those regular paths. The elk weren't a dumb class, and so they browsed along somewhere else because they were tired of getting interrupted and killed. When the bones were thrown, they pointed in random directions, and many of those directions were not going to be the same as the direction of the regular elk paths. So the elk were avoiding the regular paths and the bones were avoiding the regular paths and the Indians were avoiding the regular paths and so Indians and elk discovered each other on those random paths.

In order to convince themselves to avoid their normal habits, the Indians resorted to magic.

A famous rat psychologist has been trying for some years to conduct experiments which would show him how to raise the IQ of rats. One might wonder why he wanted to do that, considering that them rats would still be functional retardates no matter how smart they got. Nevertheless he persevered and set up lab situation after lab situation and educational environment after educational environment and the rats never seemed to get any smarter. Finally, and quite recently, he issued the statement that the only thing he could discover in ten years which made rats any smarter was "to allow them to roam at random in a spacious and variegated environment."

Explanatory Note #7

FLAX

Smiley's Bar and Bait Shop School was the only school I've ever seen in which the word *flax* was never mentioned. It was at Smiley's, by the way, that I had enrolled myself in a course called How to Survive in Your Native Land, a course invented by my friend Stan Persky in Vancouver. If it was true that I had little hope of finding out the answer, it was also true that I hoped that as long as I was enrolled I might continue to survive.

Flax is what school is all about. In my own old-fashioned geography books I went to various countries in the company of Bedouin and Greek and Turkish kids and the thing that most remains in my mind now about those imaginary kids is that they always grew flax. I myself put flax on my maps alongside corn and wheat and coal; I wrote down flax to answer questions about the products of countries. I never knew what flax was, but I knew that if I kept it in mind and wrote it down a lot and raised my hand and said it a lot, I would be making it.

Flax is actually a slender erect plant with a blue flower, the seeds of which are used to make linseed oil. Linen is made from the fiber of the stalk. I know this now because I've just looked it up in the dictionary. It is quite possible that it does grow in all those countries like the book and my test papers said. But beyond that, a thing like flax has an important place in a school. Unlike corn, say, which in L.A. we could drive out and see in fields and buy from roadside stands and take home and eat, unlike wheat or cotton or potatoes, I think you could live your entire life in America and never see or even hear of flax, never know about it or need to know about it. Only in the school, only from the geography book, only from the teacher, could you learn about flax.

It showed you how smart the school was, for one thing. For another, it showed you what Learning was; corn, for example, wasn't Learning precisely because you *could* go out and see it in the fields and buy it from roadside stands and take it home and shuck it and eat it and your mother and father could tell you about how they used to grow corn and how to tell fresh corn and about names of corn like Country Gentleman, which my father preferred. You could do all that without ever going to school and so it didn't count. Finally, it showed the school who among the students was willing and able to keep flax in mind, to raise his hand and say it aloud, to write it down, and put its name on maps. So that in the cumulative records of each child the teacher could write down for the next teacher the information that

Child reads flax, writes down flax and says flax	*Leader*
Child sometimes remembers flax	*Nice kid*
Child can't remember flax	*Child is black and/ or deprived*
Child digs flax, but inadvertently says "chili-dog" instead.	*Brain-damaged?*
Child don't dig flax a-tall	*Reluctant learner*

I think you could make up an entirely new Achievement Test, doing away with expensive and tedious vocabulary and graphs and reading comprehension, doing away with special pencils for IBM scoring and doing away with filling in all those rows. Just pass out a sheet with the word *flax* printed on it in big letters and count the seconds it took for a kid to raise his hand. That would tell you everything that an Achievement Test is designed to tell you.

Even in the Victory Gardens of 1942 America (where such an outlandish name as *Swiss Chard* became part of my experience, growing non-stop in the back yard), no one was ever known to grow flax, no one saw flax sprouting under the eucalyptus trees, no newspaper articles were written about anyone raising flax in the vacant lots, no war hero mentioned flax as contributing to the war effort. It remained, like Learning, a monopoly of the schools.

Part Three

Richard sits under a tree to my left, eating his lunch.
On a newspaper spread out in front of him lie small
roots and grasses. Look, he says, I've got twelve vari-
eties of edible plants! I taste one. It's rather bitter,
something like parsley. He names a few of them for
me, but doesn't remember the rest. How does he
know they are edible then? They might be poison,
Rich, I tell him. You might have poisoned me just
now, letting me eat that unknown plant. That tickles
him and he grins, but adds seriously that there is no
danger. He just forgot the names. But they aren't
poison. You can eat them all. That's why they are
called edible plants, he lets me know.

Chapter IX

Rabbit Mountain

A while back at Spanish Main School, it came
to pass that *Immature* was out of style, and *Non-Achiever* was in. That is what drives everyone mad at a
school, even if no one is aware that they are being driven
mad. Humans like history, like to know why things start
and end, like to have reasons for it, and the school never
has any reasons. It doesn't have any because, in fact, it
doesn't have any. But at the same time the word Non-Achiever began to appear prominently on the course
listings of S.F. State, the counselors referred to it all the
time, the teachers began using it, you could see it on cum
folders.

History *was* involved, of course. There had always
been kids in school who were smart—that is, the school
said they were smart, they could be shown to have been
smart at some time in their lives on the school's own
tests—but who did not do well in school, who got bad
grades and who were a pain in the ass. Naturally they
annoyed the school. Smart kids who got good grades were
O.K., and dumb kids who got bad grades were O.K.,
but smart kids who got bad grades weren't O.K., since
the implication was that they were deliberately rejecting
advantage, the whole notion of winning, the very virtue of
the school. If they would only try! the school would tell
the parents who came in to cooperate, and then the school

and the parents would sit down together to try and figure out how to make the non-triers try. So non-achievers weren't anything new; why were they all of a sudden so fashionable? It was simple because now History had brought about the circumstance that there were just too damn many of them. If you have one healthy non-achiever in your class who bugs you while you try to explain stuff, you can deal with him—invite his parents in, isolate him or humiliate him or send him to the office or the counselors and you get the bonus of pointing out a good lesson to your class of slaves which is worth the trouble. But get three hard-line non-achievers in there and you ain't going to be able to teach Egypt the way you had in mind because they are going to see to it that you spend all your time dealing only with them personally until you end up just throwing them out—and when you throw them out (and if you throw out three kids at once you don't look good) then the counselors have to see them and their parents and spend all their time with them and the vice-principal has to see them and spend all his time and then the principal has to and if forty teachers begin to throw out three students each then the whole school is spending all its time with them cats and so they are winning—and even then it remains the school's unshakable conviction that all kids have to be in some *room* or another all the time, even after it is clear to the school that a lot of kids ain't going to make it in rooms, since there is no other place to be in schools except in rooms. So the teacher who just threw out three intolerables gets back three more from some other teacher who also just threw out three. The school has no other ideas, and the non-achievers go from room to room, teacher to teacher, stopping by in between at the counselors or the V.P. or at Juvi, getting suspended, having parents in, coming back and ending up back in them rooms where they have proven themselves to be intolerable.

So the notion came up to have a special group of non-achievers, to be treated differently, to be dealt with outside regular school. I think the idea came from the counselors; it was supported by a new vice-principal and even by the principal, who was the same man who had taken his kid out of CA back then because it was crazy. Everyone had plenty of good motives and we spent some time together going over them. But the real reason was that the school had defined another Special Group and wanted to get it away from the regular group so that the regular group could go on doing what was right without interference. The Administrative Group tried to get Spanish Main teachers to volunteer for the job. They offered inducements; the normal school rules would be suspended for the group, the teachers would get money to spend as they liked on materials, there would be consultants for in-service, they could design their own curriculum, and, most important, they would get two Free Periods during the day instead of just one. No one volunteered. Despite the inducements, no one wanted to work with the *Achievement Block,* which was what the group got called. It was a special group; special groups in a school are wrong and everyone knew it. But the school persevered. Its mind was made up, and so it just hired the next two teachers who applied to work the Achievement Block; another man, who had worked for years in the elementary school district and who now wanted some junior high experience so he could be an administrator, was hired too. So there we were, going to have some eighty kids in the fall, do whatever we thought was Right.

We would have four teachers, five rooms in a line together. We decided that two of the rooms would be called Resource Rooms, and the other three classrooms. We envisioned paradise; the teachers would announce that they were holding classes in the classrooms and the kids would be free to come if they wished. If not, they could stay in the resource rooms, where we teachers would trade off, where nothing would be obligatory. We spent most of our three grand for resource-room materials—paints and clay and plaster and phonos and tape recorders and TVs and Bell telephone kits and science kits and games and puzzles—toys, so that while the kids were doing nothing they'd have something to do. Our main notion was that the kids didn't have to come to class unless they wanted to, so therefore when they did they would be quiet, listen, pay attention, read and work and we would have these great classes. My own vanity was that we would demonstrate how to use the school (them instruments), and give the school a lesson in change. Since we would have the kids for almost all their school day— they would take only PE and one elective, usually art or shop, in the regular school—we could really break away from its evil influence, really have school, really learn. I thought of it as a new beginning.

But in fact, the year proved to be the end of a road. The end of the road where people imagine (I imagined) that if you abdicate your total authority as an adult, then the kids will be free to choose what they want. The end of the road which says that if the adults do not make decisions about what to do, then the kids will be able to make them. The end of the road where we hoped that the students would tell us what to teach, how to teach. . . .

But the students were living in the same world as we were and lacked the same answers we lacked. They couldn't show us how to teach. Perhaps they hoped we would show them. Our classes went the same route as regular classes. Kids appeared and smarted off and disrupted things and broke the science equipment and wouldn't work. When we said, If you don't like this class why don't you cut out? You don't have to be here you know! the kids answered with familiar refrains: There's Nothing To Do Back There, or Have You Seen Mike Hunt? It was the old lesson of CA which I (being a member of the dumb class) hadn't been able to learn.

What we were doing was offering the kids an intolerable burden. We offered to make them decide what they would do. But they couldn't decide, because they had been in school for seven years and besides that knew from their lives-long all about the expectations of their parents and of the country of America. They were not free, no matter how often we said they were. No more were we. So that they *knew* they ought to go to Writing or Science or Social Studies when it was offered, because that was what you were supposed to do at school, not just goof around scattering the parts of the Bell telephone kit around the resource room while the teacher in charge pretended he thought it was a fine thing to do. But when they got there, to the classrooms, they knew too that the class had nothing to do with them, or they were afraid of it, or they would be involved in failure—that anyway it was alien to them and that therefore they were going to wreck it before it wrecked them.

I think the matter of grades is the best example. Now we were perfectly ready to abolish the whole idea of grades. No grades, we said loudly, and with perfect conviction, to the assembled group. We'd be free of them instruments of oppression. What? screamed the students, no grades? What kind of bullshit is that? They didn't want to go home first, second, third and fourth quarters without no report cards, trying to explain why they didn't have none and being called MR's. They wanted a grade in every subject, so as to prove that they were too taking them subjects, just like everyone else. Even an F was better than nothing. So we said How about we give everyone all A's? That was no good either; *if someone does work, and someone else don't, he ought to get a better grade!* Well then, we said, we'll let you guys make out your own grades; you can give yourself what you think you ought to get, what you want, what you need for whatever reason. We thought that would be satisfactory, but in fact it wasn't, because there we were, placing the burden back on the kids. So, determined that everyone would be free, we failed to solve anything that first year. We encouraged everyone to live a fantasy life, and paid the price for it in terms of a failure of solidarity. At the end of the year only Bill and I stayed on to try again;

115

the other two quit—one to teach regular science and the other to take a job as vice-principal in another district.

The school was not done with the Achievement Block though, perhaps because there were still plenty of non-achievers around, perhaps just because it existed. It persisted, and hired the next two people who applied at the end of the year to work with AB. There we were—myself, Bill, and two women, Eileen and Arpine. No four people could have been less alike. Still, in the few days we had to talk together before school started we managed to talk about our school-within-a-school on entirely different terms. It still seems to me like some sort of miracle—just like when I was a kid fishing up on Hat Creek and my father would have a limit of trout and I wouldn't be catching a one and he'd come up and say, You ain't holding your mouth right! and fish with me for a while (having nothing else to do) and I'd start catching fish without ever knowing why. We began to talk about the kids we'd have, the kids we were supposed to teach, and try to figure out what they really needed to learn. What we typically had were kids whom the school tested in the first grade and found to be very bright, leaders, reading at fourth grade level, and so on, and whom the school tested again in the fourth grade and found they couldn't read or write, their IQ's were supposed to be about 85, their parents uncooperative. What had happened in the meantime? Had they been hit by a truck? Nothing appeared to have happened, except that they had been in school four years.

We considered these questions: How come some kids couldn't learn in school? How come some other kids could? What was it that everyone in America could agree on that kids needed to learn? Why did they need to learn it, or did they? We came to no conclusion about the first questions; even though we all felt we knew all about it, all we could say was that some kids were defeated by school, diminished by it. On the latter questions we had no such problem. We had all lived in America, in the

116

West, South, Middlewest and East. No one could doubt that the parents and uncles and big brothers of every class and of every conviction in America expected kids to learn to read and write. We thought that good enough for us, and why not? Were we in America or not? Why had public schools been started at all if not to see that kids learned to read and write who otherwise—if their parents couldn't read, or if their parents were too poor to hire a tutor or couldn't teach them themselves—might not be able to do it? As for why—they needed to learn it in order to become *equal* in the country. (What else were black parents talking about when they stormed school board meetings all over the place demanding that the schools *teach* their kids and throwing out white radical educators who, in their great disappointment with America, invaded the black community hoping the black kids would teach *them* something?)

Well. In conferences and meetings and panels these past couple of years I used to talk about our school-within-a-school a lot, and what I always wanted to explain and describe was the grand feeling of solidarity we had there, teachers and students alike, for two years. I never could do it, and I can't do it now. That I can't is a defeat, and a defeat I'm now swallowing without pleasure. You readers will have to do the best you can with it as I have.

The problem is that everything we decided was a platitude and therefore hardly sounds like revelation. Our decisions, our principles (and I've no idea any more which of them got stated openly, which we just found ourselves assuming tacitly) were these:

> The school exists, and most everyone is going to go to it. It ain't going to change either, hardly. It is *absolutely irrelevant* to the lives of children, who don't need school at all, who want to have real work to do, who want revelation, adventure, who want to learn what the school is designed to prevent them from learning, who need to go up on mountains,

dream, and invent their names. There is no way to make it relevant, because it simply ain't. Public schools are irrelevant; free schools (whether invented by parents or children) are irrelevant; in-between private progressive schools are irrelevant. All irrelevant and harmful, like much else in this country, to the lives of people. You cannot sit around waiting for the revolution and doing all kinds of contemptible shit in the meantime. You can't cop out by inventing anti-schools, since you are still just dealing with the fact of school, public school, in this country. You have to decide what you are going to do now, wherever you are.

Human beings are more alike than not. What we, as adult teachers, think is important, the children probably think too.

It is O.K. for the adults to decide what's going to go on. To be authoritarian. Decide, simply because no one else can do so. What other use is there for adults, if not to decide things for kids? But you have to decide in terms of what is really necessary, not just in terms of your own convenience. You can't just acquiesce to habit, you can't just accept the decisions of dead men, and call that deciding. Your decision has got to be in terms of what everyone in the community already knows—what The People know.

We decided that we would teach reading because the kids couldn't read well, and because you had to be able to read in America in order to be equal. We decided to teach only that, in order not to diffuse things, in order not to pretend that things were important that weren't. We knew that we, The People, didn't give a damn about Social Studies or DNA or the rest of the whole kit and caboodle of junior high academics. (If a particular kid really did, he could learn about it, now or anytime.) We decided that the whole purpose of the time the kids spent with us would be to teach them to read well, and that the morning would be spent in keeping or getting their minds in shape to do it. We decided. Our risk. Our re-

118

sponsibility. Our duty, then, to figure out, now that we'd decided, how to do it.

It was then, and not before, that I began to call our school, in my own head, *Rabbit Mountain.* Rabbit Mountain was a term invented by some poets in North Beach once upon a time. Sitting in the bar, they invented a college which they were going to have. The Rabbit and the Mountain make reference to important events in their lives, and tangentially even to my own, and of course the name was thought just right for a place which would have neither rabbits nor mountains. None of those details are important here. Rabbit Mountain never existed except in the minds of all of us, and the poets have argued since, or died. But the point, the *business* of Rabbit Mountain, was solidarity. So it endures.

Me, Arpine, Bill, Eileen, Students. The counselors—Vern, Dick and Suzanne. Bruce, the vice-principal; the principal, who disliked everything we did, but supported us on every side. Judy the field-trip expert. Student teachers. David came to work at Spanish Main after it was officially all over, yet he was immediately a member of Rabbit Mountain (The People's) School. We worked, man, worked in America, in full knowledge that them instruments of repression wasn't going to be turned into instruments of love. We were members of Rabbit Mountain and we had solidarity.

With this chapter I feel like John. Now John was a kid at Rabbit Mountain and agreed to work his ass off about reading, agreed to reject his fears and desire for perfection and just try to learn to read. In the end, he really learned. That is, he ended up in the eighth grade and by pure stubbornness he could read at what the school called sixth grade level. He started off at what the school called the first grade level. So he didn't make it to what the school would call a hero of education and the school wouldn't recommend him for Harvard, very likely. It was a defeat, in a way. It was a victory too. It depends on how you look at it. I know that with this chapter I'm in the eighth grade, and only able to operate at the sixth grade level. I can't explain how it happens that you can enter Rabbit Mountain School, even though I once thought that was what the whole book would be about. You have to hold your mouth right, that's all I can say.

Chapter X

Lesson Plan

Rabbit Mountain was a morning school. The kids stuck with us for the first four (academic) periods. Then they had lunch and afterwards followed (or didn't follow) the ordinary regimen of Spanish Main School—PE, electives, and so on. We supplied obligatory Reading and more or less obligatory Math; that is, you were supposed to go to Math, but on the other hand Bill would let you out on quite flimsy excuses. Arpine and Eileen wouldn't let you out of Reading unless you were dead. So any given period would find some fifteen to twenty kids in Math, six or seven each in the two Reading classes, and the rest with me. That rest varied in number as kids visited with take passes from regular classes, as they transferred in and out of Rabbit Mountain or as their parents did it for them, or as they tried out regular classes in science or social studies or whatnot, or as they came back from trying them. We were, to say the least, rather fluid. For a student it meant that he came to school and went to Reading and then Math (or the reverse) and then to my room for two periods. Or he came to my room and then went to Reading and Math.

For people who want to talk about structure, this is a structure. I mention it because it is a way to deal with working in public schools which any group of teachers, working together, can manage. It left us free to do what we thought important. It left us free to make our own small reading classes, for instance, if we wanted to. It left us free to act on our other principle, namely to get out of Spanish Main—any one of us could get in our car with five or six kids and go somewhere any day without "permission" from Spanish Main, without filling out forms, *on impulse*. It freed us from the kind of self-indulgence where you blame the board or the administration or the country of America for your own lack of decision. In short, it freed us from the regular school structure of Noman while also liberating us from Mike Hunt and We Ain't Learning Nothing In Here. For kids are affected by structures too; I think it was clear to them at a glance that what we had in mind was necessary, reasonable and possible.

At Rabbit Mountain we offered to deal with what the school called a "problem," one which it had simultaneously invented, produced, and refused to face. From that offer we gained our liberty. When we decided to stop having an official Rabbit Mountain, it was we who decided it. We decided because we were tired of shoring up the system while it tried to sabotage us by referring openly to MR's and freaks and the dumb class. (What? We ain't going to have our experimental class no more? said the school. Our lives are not experimental, we answered coldly.) We were tired of laying the burden of being a special group onto the kids. We looked forward, with some malice, to turning loose our liberated non-achievers into eighth grade classrooms. We demanded regular classes and knew we would be able to work, to work together, in the same way. We did. We worked together, we had solidarity, we did what we had to for Noman, we did what we thought was important, we did what we thought was important to the community, and for the rest we did as we damn pleased.

Chapter XI

The Pony Express of the Silver Screen

When Red Silver came into the room you knew about it, in the same way you would know about it if a whirlwind came in. Everything was suddenly rearranged, as whirlwinds put cars on top of telephone poles or chicken coops in the basement. The desks were moved, windows opened if they were closed (or closed if they had been open), the radio turned either on or off, the back of the TV unscrewed and the image either improved or destroyed . . . he rushed through the room ringing all the changes, touching everything, and everything he touched got changed. Two minutes after he came in another kid might go over to a cabinet to get some paint and the cabinet door would fall off, perhaps mashing the kid's toe, for Red had just removed the pegs which held the hinges. Or he might suddenly be there with long nails from the shop, slipping them into those hinges on those doors from which he had slipped the pegs some other day. If you went to get a drink, the water fountain spurted out a stream six feet high and got everyone wet— or it barely squeezed out a tiny miserable trickle. Red Silver was there in either case with a mop or a wrench, doing the right thing and also doing the wrong thing, but mainly *doing*. Change! was his motto. However things were, do something to them, make them different, allow nothing to be the way it was. Red Silver was the same kid whose old man came in to see me before; the same kid who had spent the second half of his kindergarten year sitting alone in the office, not being allowed to go to class or to recess because he was so bad.

I was always trying to figure out things for Red to do besides take my room apart and put it back together again. It shouldn't have been so difficult. Red was willing and eager to do anything that "helped the school" (although the school was less than eager to do things which "helped" him), that is, anything that was real work, that accomplished something, that you could tell the difference in things when the work was done. He would help the janitor move chairs, swab floors, paint, fix broken tables. He would fix projectors, mess with TV's, help with addressing mailout letters to parents, he would have cut the grass, fixed faucets, unclogged sinks (he clogged ours often with paste or clay in order to be able to take it apart and unclog it)—but it's surprising how little of that kind of stuff there is for kids to do in a school. He didn't do "work"—that is, school work—precisely because it didn't make any difference to anything if the school work was done or not. For after it was done, either the teacher or the kid or the kid's parents (if the work got an A and thus ever got to the parents) threw it away in the wastebasket, and nothing was changed at all by it. Whether it was done or not made no difference to the world at large, except to the wastebasket and, of course, to your grade, the latter being an item long past concern to Red.

Red could have spent his time fixing up all the things there were to fix in all the rooms of the school—all the things the teachers were always complaining about—faucets, windows, desks (raised or lowered to fit kids), blackout curtains (he was an accomplished sewer), pencil sharpeners, and so on, but there was no way for a kid to roam around the school checking all the rooms for fixable items. The teachers would object to his presence, and after all their kids would be saying, Why can't we fix it? Besides, there were Maintenance Engineers who came down in trucks two months after they were called and there was a man to cut the grass who always ran the power mower past your window during the most important part of Egypt lesson and there were official Pore Kids already hired to swab the lunchroom floor for their "free" lunches.

But once, during a teachers' meeting, in a lull after some urgent talk about how to combat gum and tardiness and running-in-the-halls, came the notion that there ought to be a group of kids who could be counted on to run the projectors when teachers wanted to show movies in their rooms. Now when I was a kid, there was always a Silver Screen Club. The kids in the Silver Screen set up projectors and ran off classroom movies whenever teachers wanted them run off. They had time off from class one period a day to be free to take the projectors and the films wherever they ought to be taken, set up and show the film, rewind and take everything back where it came from. If there was no film to be shown in a certain period, they could spend their time fixing the projectors or splicing broken films or just goofing off in the Silver Screen room, a storage room where all that stuff was kept. Naturally they were all officially dumb kids and everyone knew it; who else could be allowed to miss Egypt once or twice or more each week except kids who were too dumb to learn about Egypt anyway?

Nevertheless, this idea had never come up in our school. The teachers all individualistically showed their own films, counted on themselves to run them off, signed up for and got their own projectors. The result was almost always the same; the film broke, the projectors didn't work, the teachers didn't know how to rewind the film, the kids assigned by the teachers to show the film didn't know how and wound up with *The Red-Winged Blackbird* or the *Aswan Dam* all over the floor or upside down and backwards, the sound wouldn't go or the kids fucked around with it, making it scream out one moment, whis-

per the next—the teachers, all of whom had, by Cali
fornia law, taken Audio-Visual in teachers colleges s
they would know all about projectors and tape recorder
and film strips and tachistoscopes, and so on, standin
there helpless with the film spewing out of some odd hol
in the projector while the kids yelled and laughed, finall
calling the principal, who did know all about projector
and who would fix the trouble—except that then it was to
late and there wasn't time to show the film and the teache
would be left with fifteen minutes of the class perio
with Nothing To Do, having scheduled the movie for tha
day's lesson plan—and then at the next teachers' meet
ing the principal could be counted on to deliver a lectur
about projectors and offer to give a course (after school
to teachers and kids, which no one wanted to take becaus
it was after school.

Well, this notion was brought up as if it were revolu
tionary, discussed pro and con (them kids would have t
miss Egypt) and not decided like most everything els
and dropped in favor of sticking to regulations abou
gum, which were also not decided. But I thought of Re
and the very next day approached him with this idea—
how about he got together three or four other kids an
showed them all about projectors and set up a sign-u
sheet for teachers, when they wanted what movie show
in what room, and delivered film and operator at the righ
time and right place for a guaranteed showing?

Before I'd even finished explaining all about it, Re
had picked three other kids and hustled them out the doo
and off they went. He was, as I said, quick. I heard abou
this first phase later on that day from the librarian, whos
job it was to keep and issue audio-visual equipment
What's going on? she started off by saying, and then wen
on to tell me that Red and three other kids had burs
into the library, demanded the keys to the storage room
said I authorized it, confiscated the A-V sign-up book—
it seemed like he already knew all about it, she said, h
just hopped into my back room and took it out of a
drawer, now how did he know that?—and took off. Sh

126

wasn't upset. Quite the contrary: if Red wanted to take
care of the A-V stuff, or if anyone wanted to take care of
it, she was happy to let it go. It was a pain in the neck,
she said. She knew Red anyway, having forbidden him
the library quite a number of times because of the fact
that after he left, somehow, the first kid to take a book
from some particular shelf found that whole shelf falling
down on his toe because Red had removed the pegs
which held it in place. Naturally, she said, I don't know
he did it because I never saw him do it, but it occurred
to me that he might have after he kept showing up each
time the shelf fell down, saying I hear you got a bad
shelf, I'll fix it for you—and by some miracle of coin-
cidence just happened to have some of those pegs in his
pocket. Well, she said, maybe he just always carried those
pegs around in case some shelf happened to fall down . . .
you could see she liked Red (and so I liked her) and
appreciated his spirit, say, even if she didn't propose to
have that spirit around in her library all the time.

The second phase was that I began to hear from other
teachers about Red bringing around the sign-up sheet and
browbeating (that was one teacher's term) them into signing up in advance for the projectors and the films. It
meant that they had to decide, on occasion, two or three
days in advance, when they wanted to show a certain film
that they had ordered. That was what they were supposed
to do anyway, and of course what they wrote the obligatory weekly lesson plans for, so they would know what
they were going to do for the week, each day, period and
so on, and so Red was really only forcing them into
obeying regulations. But since most of their lesson plans
were fantasy anyway, and since many of them wanted to
show the films at the last moment when it appeared they
had nothing else to do, some objected. They weren't having some kid tell them when they could show a film.
They were, though, as it turned out, for Red already
knew that all the films came in from the county office
at about ten o'clock Wednesday, and confiscated them
all, scheduled them (according to teachers' wishes if they

127

signed up, according to his own if they didn't) and
planned to show them then, in that room, regardless.
think Red saw the rooms and periods and courses and
films as parts in the inside of a TV set that didn't work
right, figured these parts out logically (and quickly) ac
cording to their relationships to each other and how they
ought therefore to work, and made plans to fix them.

On Monday the plan started out. I wasn't present
Red and the other kids had been holed up in the closetlike
room where the equipment was kept for the last two
days. Red was figuring out the schedules (and rearrang
ing the room) and the other kids were smoking, that was
how I figured it. Occasionally one of them would show
up in my room to say they were here—i.e., not cutting—
and rush back with every show of important affairs going
on. All the other kids asked Where are they going? What
are they doing? Why can't we be doing that?

The three other boys were only flunkies during the
planning phase. They didn't get to figure out the schedule
They got to smoke. Their virtue was that they knew
very well how to run the projectors and how to fix them
if minor things went wrong. Red had a supply of extra
bulbs—those little bulbs which light up when the sound
is working, and if they go out the sound don't work, those
bulbs, costing about five dollars apiece—and they got to
keep those in their pockets.

But they were the Riders. If you can imagine Red sit
ting there in his closet in St. Joseph, Missouri (not far
from Abilene, not far from Fort Kearney and Massacre
Canyon), on a Monday morning at eight-fifteen giving
the signal, and the Riders fire off on their fresh ponies
heading for North Platte, Julesburg, Ogallala, Fort Lara
mie, or Rooms 4, 25, 32, shoving those projectors already
loaded with twenty-minute films about *The Nile* or *The
Industrial Revolution* or *A Medieval Village,* running a
full tilt down the halls, the casters clattering, arriving a
the rooms (forts) and issuing orders to pull the curtains
pull down the wall maps turned backwards to serve as
screens, out with the lights and Ta-Ta! there goes the film

It goes. The Riders observe it with critical eyes. They adjust sound and focus constantly. It's over. They rush out, not rewinding, clamp on fresh film, leap to horse and down the corridors again to another room, the next film, to the cheering of crowds. They have copies of their schedules in hand, prepared by Red, who has been accused of not being able to write. They follow the charts along the Platte, past the junction of the Rio Grande, heading for South Pass and Ogden, and by noon they have each shown eight films, two twenty-minute films in each forty-five-minute period, allowing the teachers almost no time for taking roll, admonishing tardy kids, motivating the class to take note of the film, making threats about future grades, laying down rules for film watching or note taking. Teachers, Red imagines, can do that after they leave or before they come, but when they get there, Manuel and Mike and Danny, the Riders, have them fresh horses ready, saddled and bridled, sling on the mail pouches, fire up the film, thirty seconds only for the sound to warm up and away! At noon it is time for lunch, and sixth period, after lunch, it is time for the important work of rewinding the films and setting out tomorrow's schedule, time for a smoke, time to miss seventh period too, but not time to miss eighth, which is PE, which everyone hates worst of all and which no one dares miss.

Monday in the teachers' room, everyone is ecstatic. Imagine mail from New York in only fifteen days! Civilization and Progress wherever you look. How pleased they all are that Your Kids (meaning mine) can Organize Themselves for Useful Service! Manifest Destiny and All Is Not Lost. It is an argument for Technical High Schools —These Kids can Work with their Hands, give them some Responsibility, and so on.

By Tuesday afternoon things slowed down. There were few films to show that morning. Nevertheless those that were shown followed the same wild rush; Red's schedule abhorred wasted time. Wednesday new films came in, were scheduled and took off early Thursday morning for Salt Lake City, racing down the halls, bursting into rooms, cutting short opening formalities, rushing out with the projectors and films, running down the trails again . . . that afternoon the opening glow was over and I began to hear complaints. These complaints took on an odd, negative, indirect flavor.

No, they weren't rude. Polite in fact. Just . . . what? *Firm,* seemed to be it. Everything had to stop in the room when the Riders arrived to show film. I know they have a schedule to meet, but . . . No, nothing went wrong, in fact it ran beautifully and there was none of that horrible delay while we have to fix the machine or adjust the film and the kids get out of hand, and yes, it's really nice having someone competent to show it and nice that it arrives right on time. But . . . But what? Well, my kids keep asking why they can't run the film themselves (even though they've been running it for some time and still goof it up each time, I wonder if they do that on purpose?) and after they leave I have to explain why they are doing it and getting out of class and all and why my kids can't and it takes up almost as much time as when we ran it ourselves and . . . well, all of a sudden in comes this damn Danny who I had last year and almost drove me crazy and never would do any work at all even though I called his parents about every day—they never would come in to cooperate neither—and tells me it's time to show the film and I didn't expect it and told him we weren't ready and he tells me that it's time to show the film, look at the schedule . . . why didn't you sign up when you wanted the film? well, I wasn't sure when it would fit in, it depended on how much we got done, it's necessary to create the background for the movie, otherwise . . . then too, all that running in the halls just when we were trying to get the kids to Stop Running In The Halls. . . .

Thursday afternoon some kid in some class came up and *messed with the projector* just before Mike got ready to switch it on and he told the kid to beat it and the kid refused and Mike told that teacher to get her kid away from the projector and the teacher blew it and said it was her class and perhaps he ought to let someone else help with the projector, *after all it didn't belong to him,* and all the other kids in the class yelled *Yeah it don't belong to you, you know!* and after that got settled and the film was over the same kid wanted to rewind it and Mike refused of course but the teacher said Let him do it! adding, You can show him how, he needs to learn how, which was exactly what Red had forbidden Mike and Danny and Manuel to do since if everyone really learned, their monopoly would be finished but the teacher made him do it anyway, and he reported to Red and Red called all the Riders back, took all the films back to the office, stored the machines (not sabotaging any, he told me), took the key back to the librarian, threw away the schedule, and said they quit.

Halfway to Sacramento Red Silver just reined in, got off his horse, and took a taxi home.

He wasn't depressed. It had been fun, he said, starting it off, but he wasn't all that eager to just sit there in St. Joe doing the same schedule over and over again. Mike and Danny and Manuel were bugged though, because they had to return to classes and didn't get to do all that smoking or all that running down the halls lickety-split nor have those responsible executive positions. They made a stab at organizing it themselves, but argued so much about who ought to start doing what that they very soon gave it up. The school just went along as if nothing had happened, the principal was soon heard again on the subject of the A-V equipment, its use and misuse . . . but no teachers ever said anything to me about it, one way or the other.

Chapter XII

Reading in Your Native Land

A while back I got a letter from Corporal Ron Schmidt. Schmidt had discovered that there were grown men around who really couldn't read and that in fact some were in the Army and some even in his own unit right there in Vietnam. It bugged him—how could a man not be able to read? He made up his mind to teach this guy named Roy Washington. There didn't seem to be any primers around, so he and Washington started learning to read from an old paperback copy of *Cool Hand Luke*. Later on Schmidt got some grade-school reading material from his mother, who was a teacher back home.

So after a bit, Schmidt wrote, Washington was reading some and he went around telling everybody about how he could *read*, and Schmidt used to see him reading away at the notices on the unit bulletin boards, reading training manuals, shipping labels and signs. It reminded me of old Harvey, and like Harvey and me, Schmidt and Washington were pretty pleased with themselves and planning ahead.

The only trouble was that shortly after that Washington got killed in Vietnam. *Zapped* the letter put it. "I got over Roy getting it [Schmidt wrote me], but not the fact that he could not read. That's a real kick in the head; here a man dies and all that I worry about is he couldn't read before I met him."

Chapter XIII

How Teachers Learn

So in the beginning of the school year, 1968, we agreed to really teach reading. In the days before school started we—Eileen, Arpine and I—pooled our combined vast knowledge on that subject. We figured it would be considerable, and indeed it ought to have been considerable. Arpine had never taught before, but she'd just come from courses in reading and children's lit with at least one first-class person at S.F. State; Eileen had already taught reading at a number of different places; I was (since my book came out) a big-shot educator who appeared on TV and was asked to give talks on what was wrong with the schools.

In fact, it soon became clear to us that we didn't know a damn thing for sure. I mean, Eileen knew how to go in there and Teach Reading; she'd done it before and hadn't got killed or anything and she could do it again. Arpine knew a lot of books kids were supposed to like, had heard a lot about motivation, and had read Sylvia Ashton Warner. All I really had in my head, as it turned out, was that if you got a lot of books around and didn't do anything else, the kids would end up reading them. I also knew that that wasn't true. It might be true in some other situation (like in my head or in someone's else's head) but it wasn't true in this particular seventh and eighth grade school which happened to be where we were.

One or two kids would read them, one or two kids would write Fuck in them, one or two kids would throw them, and the rest of the kids would ignore them; that was what would happen right here.

After a couple of days and after a hundred coffees and a thousand cigarettes and a million words and quite a few lunchtime beers we were able to agree that we didn't know nothing. With that we all (I think) quite happily knocked it off, went home for the weekend and were ready to start.

Long after that I was at a conference with Herb Kohl, among others, and there, amidst young black and chicano kids denouncing the assembled teachers as racists and amidst calls of motherfucker and chickenshit and amidst guitars and grass and wine and people sleeping together in the grass in their sleeping bags . . . amidst all this and other cheerful bullshit (most of it arranged by Herb) down by Santa Cruz I heard Herb calmly telling a large group of teachers that they ought to be serious about their work. That if they taught reading they ought to go out and get and read everything written on the subject of reading and teaching reading; everything—good, bad, and indifferent, read it, talk about it to each other, that they ought to interiorize all these methods and theories and practicums and notions, paying no attention to the fact that, say, Max Rafferty or John Holt liked or denounced this or that, that they ought to get all the materials possible of all possible sorts, all of this while they were teaching reading classes, and that then as they taught they would have all this in their heads and at the same time be developing their own styles of how to teach, so that all this stuff would be ready to hand, to fit in whenever it in fact did fit in. That arguing about generalities about "look-say" or "phonics" was silly; that the details of either general method were useful or not depending on what shape the kid or kids were in and what they needed. That, in short, what they needed to do was get serious, by which he meant learn everything they could about what they were supposed to be doing, and then decide for themselves how they themselves were

135

going to go about it, and decide it again every day according to what they could see was going on in their classes.

What that meant was something I understood very well, I think, but somehow to hear it in the midst of all those groovy goings-on was marvelous. It was like the calm, philosophic eye of the hurricane. I think it was the last thing anyone expected to hear that day, myself included. The teachers were prepared to hear themselves denounced by the kids in familiar terms—racist, fascist, pig, lackey, co-conspirator of capitalist, totalitarian, colonialist, imperialist, and so on; and to either protest indignantly, denying the indictment, or cry to themselves, accepting it. They were prepared to hear about freedom and creativity; they were prepared to hear about openness and alternatives. They also hoped, on occasion, to get some "guidelines" (for which read lesson plans) on *how to be* open and creative and free and understanding and non-fascist, non-pig and so on.

It put me back right into the first year of the Achievement Block, before it became Rabbit Mountain. Then I'd figured to be open and creative and anti-imperialist, etc., of course. But what it all really amounted to was this: I had hoped the kids would show me how to teach. After they did so, I would tell everyone else. But by the end of that year, it was clear the kids didn't know either. Perhaps they'd been hoping all along that I would tell them. We were both waiting around. Together, we amounted to zero. So there, the next year, Arpine and Eileen and I were embarking upon the revolutionary idea that teachers ought to know something about what they were doing. And there was Herb, yet another year and a half later, allowing as how that was so. It amounted to this: *no eye, no hurricane.*

We opened up with testing the kids, determined to try everything once and for all. We had a perfect situation for doing so, for grouping them on the basis of the tests, and for seeing what difference it made, since we were able to test them all individually and handle them in small groups afterwards. We gave an Oral Reading Test, determining from it not only something called Grade Level in reading, but also fitting them into categories according to what kinds of reading difficulties they might be having—i.e., they read well but didn't comprehend, or the reverse; they misread simple words, or inserted words which weren't there, according to context; they had troubles with certain sounds, diphthongs, consonants . . . we had a checklist of this kind of stuff and followed it through. After a couple of weeks of this we had our eight groups of seven to eight kids apiece, both Arpine and Eileen teaching four periods of reading each, each group about as rightly and rationally and scientifically placed according to grade level and kind of reading problem as you could imagine, short of only having one kid in each group. At the same time we were getting these books out of the library, and consulting with the Special Reading teacher about what she'd done with many of the same kids last year and getting the district language consultant down with her advice and help with materials and methods, and interviewing salesmen who called on us with this and that workbook, machine, book, classroom magazine or newspaper, drill system, skill developer . . . we read those pamphlets and books that no one ever looks at, things like *Guidelines to Reading, Reading Development in the Elementary Child, Motivating Reading for the Underachieving Student, The Case for Reading,* the kinds of books held in state college and district education libraries with three authors (the titles of the above are all made up, since who can ever remember them?) and we read Holt and Warner again and we read Tolstoi and I hauled out Bloomfield's marvelous neglected book and we would have read *Reading, Existence and the Absurd, The Zen Method of Reading Improvement,* or *Up Against the Wall Reading Teacher!* if we could have found them. We had a bit of money for ordering stuff, and the librarian helped us go through catalogues and the principal expedited our orders and books came in and newspapers and *Scope* magazine and *Mad* magazine and *Popular Mechanics* came in and *Teen-Age Tales* came in . . . and after six or seven weeks, or maybe more or maybe less—none of us would know that now, I'm certain—we had to admit that everyone had been extremely cooperative and helpful and that we ourselves had been the same and that we had done about all we could think of to do. So in our two prep periods together, we began to try and think about everything we'd done and gotten and how it was working and what it was all about, as far as we were concerned, right now.

First of all we noticed a number of peculiar things about the testing. We noticed first of all that on the individual oral test the kids came out much lower than they did on the school-wide group test they'd been given, part of the Iowa Achievement thing. Well, that was no doubt because guessing didn't help and being test-wise didn't help, and cheating was almost impossible. But we also noticed that quite a few kids in our reading classes who the test said were reading at third or fourth grade level were in fact reading very complicated books, carried these books around in their pockets, talked about them—books like *Black Like Me,* or an abridged version of Trevor-Roper's books about the Nazis, or a history of World War II battles. It was clear they could read those books. We also remembered the results of giving each other the Oral Reading Test. That test consists of a sheet with paragraphs printed on it, beginning very easy and going up to rather difficult. Each paragraph has a few questions to be asked orally of the student after he reads it. You listen to the kid read and mark down notations of the kinds of errors he makes, then you ask him the questions about what he reads and see if he understood it. When he makes more than five errors (I think it is) on any one paragraph he is to stop, and you figure out from that his reading grade level, look at his kinds of errors and presto! he's placed.

Well, we remembered that we'd all made mistakes on the comprehension part. I made a mistake answering a question at the third grade level and two more further on. The third grade paragraph was something about a family in the park having a picnic; the mother and the father were watching the kids play and laying out the food. What are the parents doing? asked the Test. Watching the kids play, I told the Test. Wrong! said the Test, they are laying out the food! I came out to be reading at the seventh grade level.

We also felt that the test was extremely vulnerable to the conscious or unconscious influence of the test giver upon the results; that if the test giver's job or reputation depended on the kids' improvement, or if she just really wanted them to improve, it was pretty damn likely that they would improve on the test. It was also open to standard objections to testing; it told the kid, via the tester's voice, that it didn't care about speed, that the kid wasn't to worry about that and should take his time. At the same time the kid could see that the tester was timing him. It told the kid not to worry about mistakes but just do the best he could, but naturally the kid could see the tester making little marks as he was reading. Finally Arpine and Eileen knew by this time that the careful grouping, which had in fact caused us all a lot of trouble and time arranging schedules, was a complete failure in terms of its goal, leaving aside whether or not the goal was a good idea in the first place. With all, it was now clear that among say eight kids all supposed to be reading at 4.5–4.8 reading level, making errors A, B and D (but not C), there were in fact eight kids some of whom were reading all kinds of stuff, some who would only read the newspaper, some who would only read *Mad* magazine (or look at it anyway) and some who wouldn't read anything at all. Thus the test could only mean something if you never looked at the kids themselves. Once you did, you had to abandon it. It was a good lesson and I recommend it.

I suppose the point has been made—try to get hold of everything at all relevant to what you are going to do and see what's there. It sounds obvious, but in my experience few teachers do it, or even consider it. In fact, almost none of these books and ideas and materials contained anything useful at all and we speedily threw them

139

away and forgot almost all of it. What remained of this investigation were odd bits of knowledge (clues to reading problems, occasional things to try with a kid who didn't seem to be getting anywhere) which could be usefully pulled out anytime, most of which we could have remembered ourselves from our own childhood, I think . . . but it was the investigation that was important to us all, for two reasons. First, we knew we had *done* all that bullshit—we *knew* that the standard methodologies of "teaching reading" were pitifully irrelevant at best to that goal. Second, the investigation itself was a basis for our own solidarity. *We* were deciding to read all that stuff, *we* were deciding to figure out (if we could) what we were doing, *we* decided to abandon most of what we came across and that was important in a place where the people most directly concerned with children decide almost nothing about what they are going to do with them.

In the end—but that's wrong; there was never any end to it, for in our new situations now we still seek each other out to talk about kids and what's happening with so-and-so and who liked this book and . . . so, as the year went on we came to our own simple conclusions which were not anything strikingly original, to say the least, which we came to imagine everyone knew, which had been stated in many ways by people a long time ago and were being said by people right now, but which were ours, and we could state them (and more important feel right with them) and put them to use and *do* them, and that not in a free school or anything else but in a goddamn public American junior high right here and now.

Briefly, we just knew it was absurd that a normal O.K. American kid of any class or kind of twelve years old shouldn't be able to read. Why was it? Because reading is not difficult. Anyone can do it. It is an activity which no one seems to be able to explain but which everyone can do if given a chance. It is simple for people to do. If you know enough to tie your shoe and come in out of the rain, you can do it.

If you can't do it, you must have been prevented from

140

doing it. Most likely what prevented you was teaching. For one thing, if you have to get taught the same "skills" for seven years over and over again, you probably get the notion that it is very difficult indeed. But more important, the "skill" involved in reading is at once very simple and quite mysterious. Once you can look at C-A-T and get the notion that it is a clue to a certain sound, and moreover that very sound which you already know means that particular animal, then you can read, and that is certainly quite simple, even if the ability of humans to do this is opaque. What you probably need to do then is to read a lot and thereby get better at it, and very likely that's what you will do, again, if no one stops you. What stops you is people teaching you skills and calling those skills "reading," which they are not, and giving you no time to actually read in the school without interruption.

That, basically, seemed what was wrong with everything we had investigated. With the tests, with the "methods," with the class structures, with the teacher's determination to teach . . . that no one had ever had much time in school to just read the damn books. They were always practicing up to read, and the practice itself was so unnecessary, or so difficult, or so boring you were likely to figure that the task you were practicing for must combine those qualities and so reject it or be afraid of it.

I think of a normal reading class, as it was when I was in school, as it is in my own school, as it is in most schools. What goes on? The bell rings. Roll taking, admin tasks, demands for order. Speeches from the teacher, motivating the kids to read. Perhaps fifteen minutes' worth of that. Then an assignment or a few assignments, figuring that the teacher has "grouped" the kids. The kids get out the reading textbooks. Five minutes more to find the book, find the page, complain about the dumb story and ask about do we have to read this? About the time the kids are looking at the title or reading the first paragraph (or not-doing either) out comes the ditto sheet containing the real assignment—questions on the reading. Who has red hair? Why didn't the man stop after he ran over the puppy? Why did the kid ride the rocking horse? Give your opinion. Summarize the action. Who are your favorite characters? What would you have done? Or the teacher writes the questions on the board (if she has read the story herself) or tells the kids which questions to do out of the back of the book. Either way, there are twenty minutes left in the reading period and all the kids immediately stop reading the story because they know that what is important to the teacher is that they answer them questions. Naturally the teacher gives out the questions so she can check up on who read the story and who didn't; everyone then forgets that it is these same questions which have just prevented everyone from reading the story. You watch the kids stop reading and start flipping through the pages looking for the answers to the questions. Find the word *red* and near it the word *Johnny* and there you have the answer to question I; *Johnny* has red hair.

Take a look at the Oral Reading Test. Take a look at the textbook methods for Teaching Reading. Look at the books themselves. None of it is about people reading books or newspapers or magazines, but instead about Reading Comprehension. So you have short paragraphs, beginning out of nowhere and ending in the middle of nowhere, and the only reason you would ever look at the paragraph is if you have to answer the questions. The Reading Test resembles nothing else called a book; no one would look at it and think it something to read. It is full of short bursts of print, surrounded by arrows and staccato headlines adjuring you Read! Think About! Widen Your Interest! A New You! and full of red-outlined boxes with print inside them and color photos and questions about every bloody thing. Does that look like a book which you might find on a shelf or in the drugstore and look through or decide to take or read? So that even if this piece of shit does contain "The Rocking Horse Winner" or a thousand stories you might actually like, you ain't going to read it. Or if you are just reading everything in sight like quite a few kids, then in your determination to actually read the story just as if you were *reading* something, you won't have time for the questions, which will by the way seem even more stupefying if you've read the story and liked it, and you find yourself getting a bad grade in Reading, precisely because you've been reading.

There you are. All this has been, and is being said—I say it again, not because I think no one will know it if I don't, but because it belongs to the business of this chapter, which is really not about reading, but about the anthropology and politics of a school.

Somewhere along the way we knew that what we knew about how to teach reading was what our memories could have told us, what we always knew, and that was that reading is best taught by somebody who can already read and who knows and likes the kid—the kid's mother or father or uncle or tutor or teacher—sitting down with the kid with a book and reading to the kid and listening to the kid read and pointing out things about sounds and words as they go along. That in the past everyone had known how to do that as part of being a parent or an uncle or an older brother and so everyone still knew, if they just wanted to remember it. That the "problem" of reading was simultaneously caused and invented by schools and their insistence on teaching "classes" and "groups"—and by the resulting quest of teachers to find ways to "teach," i.e., ways to standardize and to measure. That there simply is no way to measure what is crucial about reading a book—namely whether or not the kid liked the book, whether he imagined himself involved in the adventures of Jim Hawkins, whether or not he was changed by it. "This should change your life," says Rilke. Who can measure that? And yet it is all that counts.

So we were caught curiously in the middle. We were in a school which hoped to measure and standardize everything, and in which the kids themselves knew that everything important got grades, could be measured and was standardized. No one was getting A's for being moved to tears when John Silver took off for the last time in the longboat. What we had to do was recreate the way of teaching reading which existed before schools were invented, and use it in the school itself. Reading not as a skill (to be measured), but as an art (that which changes). Nothing could have been simpler. Get a lot of books in the room, tell the kids to bring their own, go around during the period and sit with each kid for a couple of minutes and let him read a bit to you, read some to him perhaps, talk to him about the book and what's going on in it, point out (perhaps) this and that word, sound, and then let him go on and read it while you go over to the next one. Say over and over again—in the classroom, in the teachers' room, in your sleep perhaps—A good reading class is when the kids come in with their books, sit down and read them, and don't stop until the bell rings. Resist the urge to talk and discuss, resist the urge to watch the kids all happily working in the workbooks and programmed materials, resist the urge to motivate and to teach something to everyone at the same time, resist the urge to measure one person against another or everyone against any standard; resist every day all the apparatus of the school which was created in order to enable you to *manage* and *evaluate* a group, since it is just that management which destroyed the kids you have in your class.

You must examine your authority for what it is, and abandon that part of it which is official, board-appointed, credentialed and dead. Then you must accept the natural authority you have as an adult, belonging to a community of adults which includes the kid's parents and relatives, all of whom expect the kid to get a "good education"—by which they mean he becomes literate and equal, not that he becomes a non-reading intellectual. Your assumption must be that being literate is a human facility, and everyone can do it, and that you teach *one person at a time* how to do it if he needs to know. Then you are a teacher instead of a manager; not before.

So it was simple, and tough. Everyone always wonders

if such a way really can work (as if management does). I propose telling you flat that it does. It works if you have eight hard-line non-achievers, as our reading classes at Rabbit Mountain had; it works if you have thirty-five "regulars," as I have now. It works in the school terms— i.e., according to the standardized tests—if anyone gives a damn. It works in my terms. It works not by method but by virtue of the measure of trust between you and the student, who is very likely someone who has learned in school to avoid trust and must learn through you to accept it, as you have to learn it through him. Naturally that is tough and may indeed take most of the year. Learning to read is not tough; accepting the possibility of learning may be so for both of you. I remember students of Rabbit Mountain who were rather disappointed when they finally got it through their heads what all the fuss was about—having battled themselves for so long about reading, they wanted it, when they came to face it, to be a more heroic task.

It worked. I knew it worked because by the end of the first year I stopped hearing all those complaints about reading class. I stopped hearing kids ask me for passes to get out of Reading, to go here and there on some important errand which had to be done during reading period. I stopped hearing about how awful Eileen was and how mean Arpine was. I even heard the dreadful admission that someone was looking forward to going to Reading, looking forward to reading their book, looking forward to a little peace and quiet where they could be left alone and *do what they wanted*.

School began that next fall as if it had never stopped. We just kept on going. We were pleased with ourselves. The new kids came in and took to reading right away; they knew they had troubles in reading, they admitted it and they knew we were going to show them how to get over those problems and they wanted to and we could do it—ah, it was all clear and right. We tested no one.

We arranged groups just by taking the first eight on our list and so on down the line. We laid off the workbooks and skill books and all that and invited the kids to pick up on the books and papers and magazines in the room to take any part of them, like a crap game. Off we went.

I say we. Naturally I wasn't doing any of this. No more was Bill. I was seeing the kids in my two groups of thirty or so two hours a day. Bill had them all for math in four groups. I'd gotten together a lot of new math stuff and had some idea about Bill using it; I gave it to him, but he wasn't excited. He thought the kids needed to just do the regular school math, which most of them found simple enough. To just do it in a regular school way, without fuss and without making a big deal of it. He was probably right; it was reading which was our main thing, the purpose of the whole program. One high-powered purpose at a time was enough. But we all four sat around and talked in the afternoon waiting for our last class—our link with the school at large—and in between doing crossword puzzles and talking about Eileen's car, which was always being stolen away piece by piece from her garage and laughing and commenting about the kids, we always managed to get in a few words about what was going on with reading. It was, after all, a real question: Could you really teach anyone, or help anyone to learn something, in a public school in the seventh or eighth grade?

Now the main school had made a change this year. I had decided to start teaching reading to all seventh graders again, after a long layoff. Why it had done so wasn't too clear. Perhaps it had to do with the district-wide achievement scores which Sam, the principal, read off to us at a teachers' meeting. The kids of this advantaged district were way down below the national average in everything. They were down in math and language and social studies and in reading. Sam used to drop into the teachers' room during those afternoons and talk to us a bit as we sat there, a solid unit facing the scattered individualist teachers at the long tables. He told us that it was odd: the only subject area in which the kids did

146

well, as a districtful, was in science, and the funny thing was that science was the only subject not specifically taught in the elementary schools. What about that? he asked. We had no trouble drawing an inference there and began to yell and laugh, in our usual keyed-up way (remember our solidarity, and how little you get of that in America, let alone American schools, and you'll understand being keyed up) about how the more teaching the less learned and so on. We probably made a few uncalled-for remarks to the other teachers about how to not-teach their classes if they wanted them to learn something. Sam chuckled too, and it was the beginning of fairly regular meetings in the afternoons, Sam coming in talking about what admin job he was trying to avoid, and we telling about reading and the kids and incidentally giving a lot of advice on how to run the school. We began to feel he was on our side.

Well anyway, the school was doing what schools typically do. Seeing that they had spent the most of their money on the elementary grades on reading, and spent the most time in school on reading, seeing as how they had hired the best reading consultants and the consultants had gone to the most reading conferences and reading courses and seeing as how they had bought the best texts and supplementary texts and enrichment texts and remedial texts and spent the most time with in-service for reading teachers . . . and seeing as how all of a sudden the achievement scores told them that all of this time and money and effort weren't working at all, that the kids who were subjected to this expertise and outlay were in fact sinking lower and lower every year . . . seeing all this, they made a decision to keep on doing just what they had been doing but to do it one more year, i.e., in the seventh grade.

In the face of that, Rabbit Mountain School rather lost its head. The whole thing, we began to orate excitedly at every moment, was just what we'd been saying. We'd rehearsed our remarks for a year and now they came out easily. We became zealots. We saw that it was our historical duty to change the school. When reading teachers

147

began to be heard about that time, telling each other about how bad their reading classes were, how the kids didn't want to read, and wouldn't read and how difficult discipline was in them, and how you keep teaching the "skills" and yet it didn't seem to do any good, they still couldn't read or both, we thought we saw the system falling apart, the barricades being prepared. We exulted. Everyone was admitting failure, no one was proposing solutions. We were not failing. The way was clear for us to step in, grasp the historical moment.

Before this, we had made deliberate decisions not to be evangelical, not to bug the other teachers by proving over and over again how smart we were, not to tell them their classes and methods were humiliating and useless, not, in short, to try to convert them, and not to make them angry. Arpine in particular had argued for us to improve our "image"—we ought not always sit together, we ought not curse in loud voices, Bill ought not read aloud about Portnoy shooting blasts of semen into his catcher's mitt at the top of his voice to us in the teachers' room, we ought not laugh and yell and play games (making it clear we had plenty of free time to waste) while other teachers labored over their lesson plans and lists and grades and papers to correct—that all that was vanity of vanities, harmed Rabbit Mountain School and wasn't our point, which was to find a sensible way to work at our jobs. We'd all agreed many times, without changing our ways, but up until then we hadn't, in fact, tried to convert the school.

We had a bright moment of enthusiasm when our fervor was abetted by teachers coming up to ask our advice. They did so for the right reason, we thought; if we were able to convince our bad guys to read, they ought to be able to get their bright, achieving, average, normal, regular kids to do so. That moment was dulled shortly afterwards when it became clear that there were fundamental objections to everything we had to say.

Why are they asking us, Arpine wanted to know, if they have all these objections in advance? All their ob-

148

jections mean that they really want to go on doing just what they are doing. So why ask? I had no trouble giving a cynical answer. They ask in order to object. Having asked and objected, their honor is saved. They can say, It ain't my fault, there is no reasonable other way (if there was I'd surely do it), thus their way is O.K. and it is the kids who are at fault. Let *them* change! They were like Brecht's government which, in answer to public dissatisfaction with itself, cries out, Get a New People! Get kids in my room who dig my way of running the class, and then all will be O.K. Get them other kids (they implied) out of here.

Faced with that (and not believing my interpretation), Arpine took a big step. She went home and wrote out, on paper, an analysis of the process of learning to read, of the manner in which schoolteaching prevented kids from reading, and of the way to run an individual reading class, its goal and the role of the teacher in it. She took it to school and dittoed it off. She talked to Sam about it. She got him to agree to a meeting of reading teachers at which he would preside, citing the decline of reading achievement in the district and the school, at which the paper would be passed out, and at which she, Arpine, would try again to convince the teachers to change their ways, backed up by Sam in his role as principal. Sam was supposed, that is, to give tacit approval to this way of running a class; his informal comments to us had indicated his personal feeling that it was the right way to do things.

That meeting never came off. Two or three weeks went by and all that happened was that we began to realize that the meeting hadn't come off. We speculated about why not, but see, we were working all day, or anyway part of the day, and when we weren't we were talking together about the work and the kids or about Eileen's car, now completely stolen . . . we had plenty to do, I mean to say; we didn't have to depend on the politics of Spanish Main School in order to have something to occupy our minds. Arpine put the ditto sheet into the other reading teachers' boxes in the teachers' room one day, but that was about all we did. Something would turn up, we figured.

Toward the middle of the year (it must have been) we picked up rumors that the reading teachers had decided to try to solve their problem together. They were holding regular meetings with the principal, we heard. What did they have in mind? Well, Arpine's solution apparently not meeting their needs, it seemed they considered tracking—dividing the kids up into ability groups. That was what they were having meetings about. We began to get a little outraged, the inevitable product of unrecognized zeal. How come reading meetings were going on without inviting Arpine and Eileen? Were they reading teachers or weren't they? What was this tracking bullshit? I went into the principal's office and asked Sam politely to make sure we were notified of future reading meetings. He agreed; his attitude was one of mild surprise that such a request even had to be made. It was obvious, he seemed to say, that we'd be included, and how was Arpine's Crusade going?

I reported back about Arpine's Crusade. We all got angry. We suspected the term Crusade; it gave us the notion that Sam wasn't serious. Arpine invented the name Slippery Sam right then and there. We swore and lectured and maddened one another that afternoon out loud, for everyone to hear. In the end, we concentrated on the tracking notion. We'd put a stop to it, that was that. After all, we'd done homework. We had plenty of references to studies proving that tracking was no good. We could cite; it harmed the "high" group; it harmed the "low" group; it didn't make any difference with the "average" group. The only reason for doing it was the convenience of the adult teachers, i.e., they could then fantasy that all the kids in their class were exactly the same, give them all the same "lesson" and thus (since they were all the same) evaluate them according to a "standard" (low, average, high) which they (Noman) had invented. We decided to challenge the reading teachers to present evidence that tracking was a useful notion.

We would ask them to refer to actual studies which presented any evidence that tracking was beneficial to the students. It was a setup. We knew they couldn't do it. First of all, we knew they hadn't done any research and wouldn't do any. Second, we knew that even if they did, they couldn't come up with any research which supported their point. Third, we were elated to use their own bullshit against them . . . that is, we could use the achievement tests, the marvelous bell curves, the aptitude tests, the grades, the standards, the measurements, all those things in which they all believed but had never looked at, against them. There was no way we could lose. It was a grand feeling.

The important thing to see about this is that we were crazy. For while Rabbit Mountain was employed as described above, Spanish Main School had failed to notice our attack, hadn't shown up for battle, had in fact ignored that war and begun a different campaign. At a teachers' meeting shortly afterwards, Slippery announced casually, along with news about the PTA and some changes in bus duty, that counselors would be sending out forms to some teachers requesting the teacher to place the kid for next year's reading—i.e., high, average or low. It was simpler than the math grouping, pointed out someone, which had high, high-average, average, low-average, low and low-low. Slippery went on to say that the grouping was in preparation for the New State Reading Texts. That was the first we heard of New State Texts. (Oh! Ah! Hmmm! chorused the faculty. New texts—the state was on the job, solving problems.) Since the state had grouped the texts in about a hundred different ways, the least we could do, he implied, was to group ourselves. (That was the first we heard the texts were tracked.) He didn't seem to remember that there was any war about tracking, nor did he really need to. His tone was that Of course it was all a bother, having to fill out yet more forms, but that was part of the job and let's do it in the best spirit possible. We of Rabbit Mountain were like some Japanese infantrymen unaccountably left behind on an ob-

151

scure South Pacific island, hiding out daily, foraging by night, cleaning our weapons in a cave, imagining terrific and decisive battles any moment, seeing landing craft in our dreams—only it is 1969, the war has been over a long time, and no one on either side remembers what it was about. No one knows those warlike preparations are going on out there.

For while we were working out our two learning years with the kids, the State of California had been making arrangements with some publisher or other to print millions of books. Even before that, the publisher was gambling on the predictions of his own hired experts, whose notions were based on the observations by other hired experts of some limited behavior of small animals placed against their will in unfamiliar surroundings. None of this was public knowledge. During that two years the school noticed that test scores in reading were going down, and reading teachers were able to see that they just couldn't hack it any more. Those particular small animals had all probably died by this time. The reading meetings were being held, not to talk about how to teach but to arrange details about how to track the kids and perhaps to start jockeying around to get the high groups. It wasn't even a conspiracy; none was needed. The reading teachers just wanted to track the kids because that was what junior high schools did, and because by spending all their time planning how to do it, they could avoid thinking about what they really ought to be doing. They wanted to avoid that at all cost. The reading meetings were never public. In the middle of the reading meetings the state let everyone know, all of a sudden, that it was going to give out New Texts, that them New Texts would be all arranged into high, low and in-between, three or four different kinds of each, with workbooks, skill books and everything.

Along with that, the state had no difficulty figuring out what percentage of California school kids were bright, dumb and average (although the state didn't know any of them) and published the books in numbers to fit those imaginary percentages. It was like a miraculous intervention for everyone. The reading teachers could see that they had been doing right, since what they wanted to do fitted right in, glory hallelujah, with the state, with the experts, with the small animals who had been trial-and-errored into oblivion. The state knew that it was doing right because its experts said it was making things easier for all them reading teachers who were tracked already or were planning to track, or would now start planning to track kids. Slippery knew he was doing right because he had gotten out of having to take any stand himself. The experts gathered up more small animals, purchased from people who raise small animals in order to sell them to experts who need to get results to predict things to publishers who need to advise states that wish to provide reading textbooks to teachers who are contractually hired to measure the ability of rats to weep over Long John Silver for nine months out of every year, and they were making money and assuring themselves of continuing jobs, so they were doing right. The animals are not public knowledge, the experts are not public, the bureaucrats of the state are not public, the publishers are not public, the way of arriving at any of these decisions is not public, the authors or editors are not public (their names appear on the books but since no one reads them they are not public) and there is no one to whom you can look for an explanation of why they are doing it, no one to whom you can go up and take him by the lapels and shake him and say What the fuck are you doing? The entire thing had been done by dead men. Who done it? Noman done it.

It was no one's fault. The next time Sam came in, we tried to tell him that it was *his* fault. We told him we knew that he understood what we were talking about, that he understood the stupidity of tracking, specifically that none of his or the school's problems were going to be solved that way. We reminded him that he had said many times, right there in the teachers' room with everyone listening, that most of the things most reading teachers were doing were an utter waste of time and a hindrance to anyone learning anything. We wanted to know why he let them just keep on doing it? Why allow them to track the kids? Why let them keep the kids from reading? We told him that if he didn't *allow* them to use the texts, to track, to give out ditto sheets, to do all that stuff which prevented the kids from reading, that they would have to enter a new world since the old one was forbidden. That he didn't have to even tell them what to do but only what not to do. That would give them a chance to learn how to teach, lead to public discussion among the teachers about how to teach in the public schools in America, and (incidentally) to some solidarity among the staff. The kind of solidarity which arises among people who are seriously trying to figure out how to do their jobs. The principal, we told him, ought to provide educational leadership.

He abdicated. He said public education is a game you can't whip. You just have to play it the best you can and drink plenty of martinis. He told us the schools were too big, too centralized, run by cynical PR men, thick-headed bureaucrats, used-car salesmen, and neurotic ladies . . . it was always going to be a mess, but that if anyone got hung for that mess, it wasn't going to be him. He talked a bit more, intelligently and affably, but in the end that was all he had to say. He knew it was horseshit and he allowed that he was going to do it anyway, because that was how it was being played and because it was easier and he knew he could make it.

Right. If you don't play it smart, you might end up like Schmidt, teaching zapped Roy to read. Of course, if you do play it that way, you have to end up a zombie. You have to end up a person whom no one will take seriously. If you don't do something, I told Slippery Sam, then you have to face the fact that no one will be able to take you seriously again. Well, I regretted making that pompus remark then, and I rather regret it now. Nevertheless, that was that. You cannot use them instruments of war, repression and death to promote work, knowledge

154

and love. Fakery is fakery. Work is work. Love is love. Small animals are small animals. Dead men are dead men. None of them can be turned into anything else. I agree that it is hard lines.

Chapter XIV

The Price of Amphibians

An expression only has meaning within the stream of life.

— *Wittgenstein*

This chapter is about the fact that it is so, that an expression only has meaning within the stream of life. It is also about the logical notion that in order, roughly, to know what something is (within the stream of life) you ought to be able to know what would be the case if it were not.

Alienation is such an expression. Within that particular tributary which is a school, it has the meaning that an individual gives up his Self (denying what he knows to be so in favor of what the school says is so) in order to achieve success and avoid failure. Of course, success and failure are expressions too and only have meaning within the stream in question, but by the time anyone remembers that, he is usually forty and reduced to writing about it.

For my students, and for myself, this alienation from ourselves means in practice that they (we) do or don't do things as a matter of reaction—as if we came in to school each day as so many blanks, having wiped ourselves clean of desire between breakfast and getting off the bus or out of our car. We turn ourselves off as I turn off the car radio just when the front wheels hit the curb at the teacher's parking lot. Once officially in the school we dispose of our cans of Coke and our smokes and await the presentation of our daily (streams of) lives by the school, and it is to that presentation that we respond. React. We don't act first ourselves, and let the school respond (while we watch it), for the reason that we are alienated (as presupposed) and because we are sane.

What would we be like (what would be the case) if we were not? Not alienated. From ourSelves.

In September of 1967 I looked through the cumulative folders of the kids we were going to have at Rabbit Mountain for the coming year, that is to say, the next Monday. I read what I already knew—the first grader with testable high IQ, the remarked bright student, leader, reads-at-third-grade-level, headed for the big time; and the fourth grader with low-average capability, IQ 89, lazy kid, must-be-pushed-to-achieve, reads-at-second-grade-level, discipline-problem, parents cooperative. The first grader and the fourth grader are the same kid.

I was not prepared for the phrase *identifies with amphibians*. The rest of the remarks on this kid's folder were indefinite. It was as if the folder was composed entirely of question marks. *Lazy, bright, success, leader, follower, reading level, achievement, cooperation,* apparently didn't come into it, so the teachers wrote what amounted to nothing. Only the one teacher, having written out (I imagined) some thirty such folders before, bored and maddened by the effort, had torn this one remark out of the systematic abstraction of the school's nature. It was as if, in the middle of the seventh grade social studies book about the amount of flax cultivated by Palestinian Arabs in their refugee camps, I could come across a page from *The Golden Bough* or an engraving of a priapus.

Monday mornings on the first day of school all kids come in and sit down to await announcement by the

157

teacher of their daily lives in that class, that period. It is
surprising how beautiful they are, even as blanks—or as
they wait, filling in the blanks with future re-actions as
you talk—and all the teachers every first day are full of
enthusiasm and even hope, as if they finally had gotten a
Good Class and now, they seem to say, Watch me teach!
Richard didn't come in and sit down and await anything.
He came in the door and straight up to me, smiling and
holding an eight-inch brown-backed yellow-bellied water
dog out to me in his right hand, saying Did you ever see
a water dog before?

A water dog is a kind of newt or salamander common
to all warm-water California coastal streams. I used to
catch them all the time. Its skin is sandpapery. Perhaps
it gets its name from the fact that its visage seems not to
be reptilian but gives an odd impression of warm-blooded-
ness—you get the notion, if you hold a water dog, that it
likes you. If you go underwater in streams like the
Navarro you'll see them in deep holes, legs outspread,
sinking slowly towards the bottom from which, when they
reach it, they will push off and swim upwards, orange-
bellied, towards the surface. They are amphibians.

Richard was a medium-sized twelve-year-old boy with
a pleasant face, a wide smile, a blue jacket zipped up
all the way. After showing me the water dog and telling
me where he got it, he went back to the cabinets and
began looking around for something to put the water dog
in. While I called the roll and mispronounced names he
found one of the aquariums and ran some water in it and
put the water dog in it and while I talked about the school
and its formalities he went outside and came back in with
some rocks and some dirt for the aquarium and then he
watched the water dog swim and crawl around. He took it
out a couple of times and held it, but he didn't do any
landscaping on the dirt and rocks because he knew the
water dog didn't give a damn about that, and he didn't
give a damn about that. He didn't make any noise and
didn't disturb anyone, but all of us felt how utterly wrong
his entire behavior was, since I was there in front of the

158

class talking and they were sitting down pretending to listen and he was wandering around inside and outside with dirt and rocks and fooling with the water dog and all of us wanted to do it too and so we knew it was wrong. He didn't seem to be listening to what I was saying but when I got to the part where I explained that if you were absent you had to bring a note the next day, or if you were leaving school to go to the dentist or something you had to bring a note and give it to the health office, Richard raised his hand. What about, he asked, if you were going to your psychiatrist? Well. That told us all we wanted to know. The water dog, roaming around, that dirt, wandering in and out, not sitting down—things all the kids would be doing or wanting to do all the time, but which no one would do on the first day. We were dealing with a nut. That made it easy to understand.

I've always wondered what made Richard ask that. He never again referred to any psychiatrist or to therapy or anything of the sort. Perhaps he really wanted to know if the procedure was the same. I don't know.

For the first weeks of that year, Richard got along very badly. Everything he did seemed to be odd and not with it—everything he did got to be the focus of everyone's resentment and terror in the first few weeks of What To Do? In a very direct way he was ruining me as the teacher, or in the way I was trying to work with the kids as their teacher. That is, the kids attacked him precisely where I couldn't stand it, as if they (the other kids and Richard) had conspired to involve my personal terrors from the start. The kids attacked the water dog, they attacked Richard, and they revenged themselves on the thin black blind worm-salamanders which he brought into the aquarium, dive-bombing them with rocks, putting them on the heater, throwing them against the wall.

They attacked things he made. We had a big box of wood scraps from the shop and of beautiful odds and ends from a picture-framing shop and everyone was gluing them together with white glue and making constructions. But

159

whereas everyone else made abstract architectual monuments (having already been to school art classes where any image of the real had been forbidden for some years) Richard preferred to make little toy trains and streetcars and tracks for them and then he played with them. He didn't play with them for long though, for the kids smashed them almost as quickly as he made them, threw them, stomped them, broke them, laughing and with anger.

Richard reacted to these acts with squeals of rage, with tears, with demands to me. He made placards from construction paper on which he wrote appeals to public opinion and to authority in the form of the vice-principal:

> Some kids in the eighth grade, like [followed by a list of names] are wrecking trains made by Richard S. All people in the school must get together and beat them up so they can never do it again.

> To the V.P.! Cruelty to animals is against nature. These kids are killing salamanders by heat and by bombing with rocks. They are [list of names]. Call them into the office and suspend them for ten days.

He taped these placards up on the walls of the room, he put them up in the halls outside, he hung them in the office, he even took them into the V.P.'s office and put them on his desk. The placards drove the other kids wild. They couldn't stand to see their names up there in public association with cruel acts, and they were really afraid that the V.P. *would* call them in, *would* suspend them, *would* call their mothers (it was the beginning, I can see now, of Richard's magical power) and so they tore the placards down, they threatened Richard, they hit him, killed the water dog, approached me with demands.

In the middle of all that, Richard displayed another eccentricity which provided excuse for revenge—namely, he had a great love for a kind of small-time obscenity. It mainly revolved around the word *dick*. (He never said any of the other common kid swear words; he said fucking, but never fuck, and he only used it to mean actual intercourse, never as just another vulgarity.)

So anyway, my memory has an image of Richard in an ebullient mood, having forgotten for the moment about cruelty, going around to kids talking about their dicks, and inevitably being persuaded by boys to go up to the girls and say something dirty. What Richard usually said was *Take out your dick!* The girls, the very same girls who were saying all the words Richard didn't say all the time and writing Fuck and Fuck you and Let's fuck in lipstick on the walls of the girls' bathroom, reacted with indignation and slapped Richard and made demands of me. When I foolishly told them to forget it, they counterattacked by going to see the V.P. and telling him (with what mixture of sexuality and prudishness can be imagined) about Richard told them to take out their dicks, and so he called in Richard and talked to him warily about dicks and girls and forbade Richard to say dick . . . and of course this counterattack enabled him to totally ignore Richard's own public complaints about kids who tortured amphibians to death and broke things you made, for somehow that didn't count alongside some nut or freak kid who told girls to take out their dicks! That was something you could get involved with! That you could take seriously! But dead salamanders, well . . .

(See man, this is what an American public school *is*. Let's cut out talking that shit about curriculum and learning about flax and all. The above is a School. Get it through your heads.)

All of this put me in the middle. I had to get mad at the kids who bombed the salamanders. I had to get mad at the kids who broke Richard's stuff. I had to discuss the phony outrage about dicks. I had to hear from the V.P. about should Richard be in EH classes. The worst thing was that my anger was real. I felt capable of killing a kid who stood there laughing while a moist salamander fried on the heater. I did hate the chickenshit

161

girls. And I also began to hate Richard for his utter childishness, his ignorance of what the other kids were up to, his failure to respond as a twelve-year-old ought, his total remoteness from group custom and behavior. For, instead of staying neutral (which was my plan) while the kids sweated out the crucial problem of Who Are We In This Room and What Shall We Do, I was being forced into the position of forbidding stuff all the time, of threatening, of being angry, or moralizing. It didn't matter, somehow, that it was real—that is, I really did think the killing and breaking was wrong. It didn't matter that I really thought everyone should be able to tolerate Richard. And it especially didn't matter that what I was really furious about was true—that they were attacking Richard as a substitute, as an excuse for not attacking those things which were at the root of their anxiety and frenzy, but which involved some risk in attacking, namely their parents and teachers and their lives at school eight hours a day.

So it was really quite nutty. On the one hand, I kept wishing Richard would start building abstract junk, call people assholes when he thought I wasn't listening (or deny it if I heard it), pitch pennies against the wall, smoke in the bathroom, break other kids' stuff or throw chalk, torture the water dog, make hip teen-age sexual innuendo to the girls, complain about mean teachers and grades and that he wasn't learning anything, and speak sagely of marijuana, using the words *pot* and *lid* a lot . . . in fact, become just like the other kids. Then I could *work with him, straighten him out,* get him to face his *real situation*—in short, do what I was ready to do, what the class was for, what I figured to do with the group. What was that? Why, merely to force them, through my existence in the room as *person* rather than giver of daily streams of life against which to react, rather than as successful or unsuccessful entertainer, to decide the course of their own lives.

On the other hand, that goddamn Richard was already at the point I hoped the other kids would reach. He already knew what he wanted to do, every moment of the day, he was prepared to do it, and could do it, did do it, liked to do it, it harmed no one, it wasn't isolated from his total life (he continued at school the things he did at home), he used the school's resources (science books, films, maps, geographics, aquarium, dirt and rocks) —he knew what he wanted, learned from it, required no instruction, shared his knowledge and experience, asked advice . . . he was there! It was great! It was also intolerable, because he was nuts. No one planned to put up with a nut who was also content. He wasn't alienated. No one could stand it. He was fair game.

Then changes began to happen. Richard made some of them. He stopped building trains and stuff. He didn't bring any more salamanders or water dogs. He began to concentrate on drawing cartoons and drawing maps. He made the cartoons on ordinary school paper, and the maps on huge pieces of butcher paper which he got from the office. They had a weird kind of association. The maps covered eight-foot-long pieces of paper with streets, freeways, alleys, telephone poles, street signs, street lights, bridges, underpasses, streetcar lines, depots, bus stations, bus stops, train stations and airports. The main characters in the cartoons were automobiles—generally old, famous makes like Duesenberg and Rolls ("Hey, Duse," a Rolls would ask, "What happened to you?")—and talking fireplugs and talking telephone poles and talking buildings, plus an occasional human who was usually identified as one of the members of the class or as myself and who had a bit part. Events in the classroom always played a role—someone who had attacked Richard found himself being run over by a Duesenberg somewhere in the cartoon, for instance, and when a lot of kids began to play chess later on, talking chesspieces began to enter into the action.

In itself, this changed nothing. The cartoons and maps only emphasized what everyone knew—that Richard was a nut and a babyish nut to boot. He kept wanting to show them to everyone and everyone kept being disgusted and upset. His writing, for one thing, was quite illegible; it was

163

too large, too crowded, didn't go in a straight line. (The school nurse, confronted with some of it, wanted to talk about brain damage.) He writes like a baby! everyone wanted to say. That didn't matter to Richard, since he wanted to read it out loud to everyone anyway. (Looked at from this standpoint, it was rather literate, involved somewhat sophisticated puns and was at least as interesting as the average comic book.)

The change had more to do with Tizzo and Junior and Karl, who were the Big Three of the class, and who had a certain identity in the school as a Big Three. It's odd how these combinations occur among kids. The three were in no way alike and there seemed no objective reason for either their association or their identification as a unit. Perhaps it was a question of superlatives. Tizzo, for instance, was the toughest kid in school, with the possible exception of one other boy. (All year long kids tried to instigate a fight between the two, but it never happened.) Karl was the hippiest kid in school, in the superficial sense of hipness which prevails among twelve- and thirteen-year-olds. He had the longest hair, knew all the music, associated with musicians (but did not play) and was one of the few kids (at that time) who actually smoked, rather than just talked about, grass. Junior could only be called the charming-est, or perhaps the carefree-est. He was beautiful, for one thing—dark curly hair, an open, friendly face, smiling, unworried, not angry, expressive of some term like happy-go-lucky.

In their relations to the school, they were equally diverse. Tizzo was a kid from an earlier age and another place. He didn't criticize the existence of the school, didn't question the rightness of its principles, didn't object to his place in it, which was to get (as he saw it) average grades (not too many D's and F's) and stay out of trouble. His trouble was his great anger at injustices within the system, as they affected him. He took it for granted that teachers were mean (else how would they control guys like him?) but there were limits. If a teacher didn't let him out of class every day to go to the bathroom (and

164

have a smoke) that was reasonable; if the teacher never let him out, or gave him moral lectures when he asked, that was unreasonable. If he didn't try in a class and got an F or a D, that was O.K. if he *tried* (at least sometimes) and still got an F or D, that was unreasonable. When it was unreasonable, he got angry, slammed books, cursed the teacher, hit other kids, and got in trouble.

Karl was a critic. His aim was to get out of school as soon as possible. He wasn't concerned about degrees of things. He resented being made to go to class and was uninterested in whether the teacher was good or bad, nice or mean. His goal was the Continuation School, where his older brother had gone and where all the hip kids went (according to Karl), where they let you smoke in class, and where you could learn what's happening. He constantly criticized the structure of the school and the curriculum. His grounds for discontent were that it was useless and irrelevant. His philosophy was direct and simple, and also typical; he did nothing to hurt anyone else, therefore he should be allowed to do as he pleased. It was his business; he had nothing to learn from anyone.

Tizzo and Karl, however, both attended regularly, Tizzo in order to keep out of trouble and stick to his Roman sense of order, and Karl because only at school could you get a sizable audience for existential criticism of it. Junior, by contrast, came when he felt like it, almost always late, sometimes not at all My image of Junior is of him coming in the room at eleven and saying that he thought he'd drop by for lunch. When he dropped in, he was immediately the center of attention. What did you do all morning? everyone would ask. Well, Junior hadn't done anything. I just watched Captain Kangaroo, he'd say smiling, and then I went back to sleep and got up and ate some stuff and got dressed and thought I'd come on over here for lunch. Hey, Mr. Herndon, he'd say, can I go out to the bathroom? And then Junior and five or six other lucky kids would go over to the bathroom and smoke and talk until lunchtime. I always felt good when Junior wandered in, and so I knew the kids felt it also. It was good to have him around (that's all you can say), you missed him when he wasn't there, and that was his superlative quality.

I want to remark here about fathers, or upon the absence of them. Unlike black inner-city ghetto pore deprived (choose your term) schools, most kids officially had fathers in our district, but in fact fathers were rarely mentioned. Kids talked about mothers. It was mothers they tried to satisfy, mothers who got mad if you got in trouble, mothers who came (with few exceptions) to the schools, mothers who wanted you to get good grades and go to college, mothers who wrote you fake excuses (like Junior) or who you didn't want to feel ashamed of you (like Karl). I think I can tell a kid who has a real relationship with his father within a week of having him in class, it is that unusual. The point, for the present story, is that Tizzo was such a kid. He had an Italian father. His father was (according to Tizzo) rough and tough and would beat the hell out of him if he got in trouble. He wanted to avoid it. His father thought he ought to go to school, be clean and neat, get there on time, not smart off to the teachers, and not flunk. Period. Tizzo had a lot of tales about how strong his father was, even though he was smaller than Tizzo, who was at thirteen already a man physically, being about five feet ten and weighing perhaps a hundred and seventy. He also had a lot of tales about working with his father, going around with his father, fixing up the house with his father—in short, of manly relations with his father. In fact, he was learning how to be a father himself. He knew what his father did at work, what he did at home, what he thought, and how to please him. His concern was uncritical. His father was right, his demands not impossible; he Tizzo was imperfect and couldn't always control his temper and when he couldn't, deserved to be punished, deserved his father's anger, deserved to have to stay home instead of spending the day fishing for striped bass off the beaches of San Francisco. He didn't like the punishments, he thought the school could let up on him a bit and didn't have to be quite so tight, and he hoped continually for a break, a little luck in getting through, but he didn't criticize its general right to exist.

So the Three approached me one day. All of a sudden they were concerned about Richard. All these other little punks keep picking on him, they told me, and they had decided to do something about it. Richard has a right to exist even if he is nuts. He isn't hurting anyone else, said Karl, and so he has a right to do his thing. And everyone picks on him just because they are chickenshit, said Junior. They pick on him because he can't take up for himself, and because Richard is so nutty that the vice-principal won't do anything to them when they bug Richard, cause he thinks it's all Richard's fault because he is so crazy and tells the girls to take out their dicks. Tizzo said, They do it because they can get away with it!

So their analysis was that all kids would torment anyone and anything if they could get away with it. The only reason kids would act decently towards other creatures was if they were afraid of punishment for acting otherwise. That was what their lives, in and out of school, had taught them. They didn't treat Tizzo badly, because they were afraid he'd beat the shit out of them. They didn't treat Karl badly, because he'd put them down for being wimps and had the reputation to make it stick. They didn't treat Junior badly, because then he wouldn't smile at them and ask them to come along to the bathroom. Richard, having no saving graces of that kind, and having no protection from adults because he was nuts, had to take it.

Tizzo et al planned to turn things around. They proposed to supply the punishment to any kids who *bothered* Richard. Well, I said O.K. Why shouldn't I? It was a step in another, if not the right, direction. It also meant that Tizzo and Karl, who had been (to be honest) among Richard's chief persecutors, wouldn't be doing it any more, and that would be a break for Richard.

It became, immediately, an instrument of terror. All the kids became fair game themselves; they were in the same relationship to Tizzo and Karl and Junior as Richard had been to them. As soon as they had conferred with me, the Three foraged out firing on kids. They belted them for what they'd done a week ago to Richard, for what they'd told the V.P. a couple of days ago, for what they were planning on doing to Richard tomorrow. The three were full of anger. They hit half the kids and threatened the rest. If kids who were physically (if not morally) tougher than Karl or Junior protested, they were confronted with Tizzo. Girls, who were not to be hit according to Tizzo, were made to sit down in desks and not move. (If they moved, they were hit anyway. It was their own fault; they were told to stay put.)

We spent perhaps a week under the Terror, a week of outcry and protest and attempted discussion. Why was I allowing goon squad rule?

Why are you tormenting Richard?

How come Tizzo et al, who had been tormenting Richard, were all of a sudden allowed to hit kids for tormenting Richard?

How come you are all tormenting Richard?

How come we have to have some nutty kid in our room?

How come you bomb water dogs?

How come Richard get to tell us to take out our dicks?

How come you want to write Let's fuck! on the bathroom walls?

How come Richard has to make all that nutty stuff?

How come you care what he does?

How come Tizzo and Karl and Junior, who are part of us, i.e., our leaders to whom we look up, turn against us when all we are doing is exercising our normal white sane American middle-class, or almost middle-class, prerogative of tormenting anyone and anything that isn't clearly us and tormenting it *without any fear of retribution?* What other good reason could there be for remaining this normal white, etc., with all its load of fear, guilt and alienation, than daily assurance of this reward? Why, consid-

ering our own agreement that everything we want to do
—everything from writing Fuck you to talking to each
other in class—is wrong and deserves punishment, ought
some kid to be doing whatever he wants and think it is
O.K.?

After about a week, the Terror began to peter out.
Junior, having come to school regularly and early in order
to keep Ordnung, began to arrive at noon. Tizzo and
Karl found their interest beginning to flag. Perhaps they
had only wanted to re-establish their Big Threeness in
concrete terms; having done so, they didn't figure to keep
up this eternal slugging. They weren't cruel, only angry.
Still, it worked, in a way. Prevented by the goon squad
from pinning the sins of the world on Richard, the class
began to look elsewhere for something to do.

In the meantime, Richard, left relatively alone, had
not been idle. He began to exploit his three major apti-
tudes—natural history, maps and magic. Indeed, he began to gain grudging admirers. He scoured the library and
came up with fantastic photos of snakes devouring other
beasts, or magnified tarantulas' jaws, or piranhas, cobras,
moccasins and other death-dealing reptiles. No one could
resist them. Since Richard was the only kid willing, at
that time, to do the work necessary to produce this fas-
cinating material, everyone had to gather around him in
order to look, everyone had to hear his stock of snake
lore and no one could just snatch the book and run and
look at it by himself because of the Terror.

It was the same with his maps. He had begun to make
huge maps on fifteen-foot lengths of butcher paper. To
his great pleasure and astonishment he discovered that the
school could afford butcher paper, as much as you wanted,
in whatever lengths you wanted, as often as you wanted.
Life was good. He spread the paper out on our long
table, the ends drooping over, and covered it with freeways, overpasses, bridges, streets, alleys, stop signs, turn
offs, thoroughfares, bus stops, streetcar tracks, depots, and
the rest. Up until this time, we had all figured it was

fantasy; our judgment was variously that it was interesting or nutty or disgusting but, either way, predicated on the fact of fantasy. When it was discovered that it was not fantasy, it was like revelation. How that happened I'm not sure, but, in any case, I recall kids coming up to me and saying that goddamn Richard says his maps are real and what did I think of that? So for a while we all stood around interrogating Richard about maps. Sometimes he was eager to answer—to trace the beginnings of a freeway in South San Francisco and show where it went, where bus connections could be made, where turnoffs to Tierra Firma could be expected—but at other times he displayed irritation, an irritation directed at dilettantes who were (1) not serious and (2) *bothering* him by getting in the way of his work. Still, he was convincing. If a kid asked, Rich (all of a sudden it was Rich, not Richard-you-nut), how would you get from here to Haight-Ashbury (mentioning one of the few places in the city that all the kids had heard of), what bus would you take? then Richard would stop working and get serious and answer the question in detail; what jitney to take, where to get off, what number bus to get on then, what street to transfer at, where to get off and then walk two blocks north . . . or kids who had once lived in San Francisco would say, Look, Rich, I used to live at such and such a street, number so and so, tell me what bus goes by there and where it came from and where it goes. Richard would think a bit and then say, Well, it would be Muni bus Number 48 (or whatever) coming from . . . and then go ahead and trace the entire route of the bus, street by street, finally allowing the bus to go right past the kid's former house on its journey into the mysteries of the city.

Then Richard's maps, having the decisive quality of the real, began to attract co-workers. It turned out that Richard was not against having houses drawn in on streets, or Doggie Diners or movie theaters. So that one morning I was treated to the sight of a bunch of kids sit-

170

ting by the table over Richard's map, eagerly drawing in Martin's Travel Agency, Holt's Conservatory, Kohl's Burlesque (20— girls—20), Grand's Nursery (Exotic Plants), Stroud's Orpheum and Foundation, Spino's Health Farm, Perry's Gym, and so on. Other kids rushed me with demands for pencils, pens, marking pens and crayons and I got in a little sarcasm about *students* being *prepared* for work but in the end, not being prepared with any such items myself, had to send to the office for them. For I too had plans for Richard's map, and spent some time later elbow to elbow with kids (Move over! I can't move over, I'm drawing right here! Well I got to have room to draw! Well, I have to have room too!) drawing in Herndon's French Restaurant, a medieval affair with towers and moat and an immense menu featuring Sole Margeury with Petits Pois, which (I admit) was much admired.

Thus did Richard triumph momentarily over us all, a triumph in which we were happy to acquiesce. Richard's (now our) map was completed in perhaps a week and was hung up on the wall and admired, not only by us but by counselors and administrators and art consultants and visiting firemen from San Francisco State. It had a Fillmore district with soul food and dance halls and it had a Chinatown with opium dens and curio shops and it had museums and movies and Aquatic Park with bongo drummers and naked-lady sunbathers and it had a Haight-Ashbury with poster shops and drug emporiums and it had suburbs with shopping centers and houses with the kid's names on them and police stations and a gigantic Juvenile Hall with guard towers and machine guns and a big sign out front which said Junior's Juvi.

All in all it was pleasant to come in and watch fifteen or so kids sitting along the table opposite space on the map, drawing and coloring and looking at one another's stuff. Naturally we had incidents. There were bad guys who wanted to write Fuck on the map, and there were objections to the tyranny and unfairness of Richard, who, acting as Planning Board, allotted drawing space accord-

171

ing to some design in his mind not readily apparent to the rest of us. There was also some outcry about Richard's naming of the streets (a job he allowed no one else to do) wherein inevitably some kids had major freeways named after them (Tizzo Memorial Parkway) and others were only allotted minor streets or even alleys. Still, the map was finished, with an awful decrepit falling-down tenement named after the vice-principal, located on a tiny alley of the same name which was carefully decorated with garbage cans, old whiskey bottles and refuse. Two days later Tizzo got mad at Richard because of the Memorial Parkway. Some brave kid had pointed out to him that *Memorial* meant that he, Tizzo, was dead. What the hell, Rich, I thought I was your friend, said Tizzo. Sure, Tizzo, said Richard, you are. But that map's in the future! It's all in the future.

I doubt that Tizzo was satisfied by that answer, but all he could do about it was to remember some kid who had written a passing Fuck on the end of the Parkway and threaten him a bit.

Richard was probably the only kid who was not completely satisfied by the map. I could see he liked the attention and the unaccustomed feeling of working with other kids on a project of his invention. At the same time, he made it clear that they *bothered* him. He had to keep watch over them so that they didn't encroach on space he had allotted for something else. He had to argue with them about details. He had to take them into account, and that was a *bother*. More important, I think, he had to compromise his idea of reality—the map was now clearly a fantasy, could only be a fantasy, at best something of the future. It *might* come true; that was as close to the real as Richard could make it.

I said magic. Free of persecution and momentarily full of power as Director of Map Activities, Richard indulged himself. Kids began to rush me with complaints in a new key. Tell that fucking Rich to stop turning me into a frog! Richard said I was turned into a fart! He said I am immobile!

172

It's true, ain't it? I remembered to answer slyly. It's true, you *are* a frog, a fart, you can't move! No it ain't, they said, of course it isn't. What are you worried about then? I would say. But they *were* worried. Richard had them in the old grip of the Logos, and they genuinely didn't want him to do it.

The ritual was simple, Richard would come up to kids, walking on his toes and grinning with secret delight as usual, and ask them Say Om. (Or Say X or anti-disestablishmentarianism or Shazam.) The kids couldn't ever resist and so they'd say it. Then Richard would say, You are now a frog, or Now you don't exist. Then the kids would disprove it (they hoped) by running hollering to me. They were prevented from solving it more simply by the memory of the Terror.

I enjoyed this action quite a bit, but in the end I could see everyone was really quite bugged and I began to tell Richard to lay off. I expected it to be difficult. All of a sudden we were some nomadic tribe caught between Attila-the-Big-Three and Richard-the-shaman. We alienated folk were in danger. I called Richard over and began to explain why he had to stop turning everyone into frogs. But Richard just said, innocently and quite reasonably, After all, Mr. Herndon, it's only a joke!

It was as if that remark, turning us almost against our will away from our urge towards supernatural explanations of all our difficulties, loaning us sanity and the real, just as mothers soothe their children at bedtime by telling them that TV program, that Monster, Vampire, The Glob, Murderer, they aren't real, they are just stories, they are made up, just pretend . . . the kids still have nightmares, of course, since nightmares can't be done away with by applications of reason like wet compresses, but they can be recognized and talked about as nightmares, given a name apart from breakfast or play or sunshine . . . as if that remark turned us off of Richard, diffused our focus on him, and let us back into our own lives in the classroom. Most likely, of course, it wasn't that at all, there

173

was no actual moment of turning away but only some gradual release, unclear as to its moments, from our obsession. But memory wants to pinpoint its feeling of history, so as to make art. (The Muses are the daughters of Memory.) We began to go our own ways, ways which only occasionally touched Richard's or his ours. Kids occasionally did some drawing on Richard's maps. I occasionally stapled his cartoons up on the board alongside other stuff. Richard occasionally gave informal lectures on the habits of amphibians. When a group of kids developed a flourishing business making ceramic chesspieces he joined them, but not as a co-businessman. He made his own clay chesspieces alongside them, using the same clay at the same time, but that was all. His knights looked like sea horses, his pawns like tiny fireplugs.

The year went on. Richard wasn't the only kid in the class. Maps were not the only projects. Salamander torturing wasn't the only barbarism. Richard's mother came to see us a couple of times. She reminded us all of Richard; she gave the impression of being too placid, perhaps a bit vague, not worried enough. Naturally we had to see her in contrast to the mothers we usually saw who were mad for success, were outraged or wept, wanted to settle and fix everything in their kids' lives in half-hour conferences on their way to afternoon league play at the bowling alley. She mainly hoped that he would make some friends. She was happy with our program without knowing or caring to know much about it since Richard told her the school didn't bother him. I got a few calls from Richard's therapist, who wanted to know how he was getting along. It became clear that the therapist saw Rich as a pretty hopeless case, i.e., that he was never going to be a "normal" kid, that the best that could be hoped for with all the therapy in the world was that he could keep out of an institution and perhaps hold some kind of job like the ones social workers invent for severely retarded adults. Later in the year I worked up courage enough (and believed it enough) to tell the therapist about Richard's real ability and, more important to him (for Richard's intelligence didn't seem to him to be the issue so much as what he could *do* with it), about his actual acquired knowledge of the real world in concrete terms of geography and science. I told him I thought that if Richard could get through the age of being a kid and a teen-ager without being physically or spiritually murdered, that he might emerge (to a startled society composed of the therapist and ex-classmates and aging teachers) as a perfectly reasonable thirty-year-old citizen, albeit a bit eccentric like many another citizen, working at some fairly unusual job, one which very few other people could do. The therapist seemed to like the idea and in fact we both got a little excited about it then and there. He seemed to have visions of museums and classifying salamanders. I thought about the post office, where I used to work, and the difficulty of memorizing mail-routing schemes, the contests in the coffee rooms among supervisors and old hands about where certain streets were, what they used to be called, what routes served them, and so on, and I conjured up Richard, the Grey Eminence of the P.O. in a dusty back office drawing charts and schemes, settling disputes and reading the archives. In fact, when I thought of the future of America in terms of science-fiction (the predictions of which I always believe), I rather thought that Richard was one of the few kids in the class who had any real chance of having a job, of having work to do that a machine couldn't do and wouldn't be doing. Richard and Junior, by the way, whose uncle was a bail-bondsman.

P.S. Because the rest I write about Richard appears here like a postscript. Of course it ain't a postscript to Richard, or to Tizzo or to Richard's dad, or in fact at all to anyone, really. Readers ought to beware of the trouble with books. Still later in the year Richard's mother came to see us again, and she was quite upset for the first time. Richard's dad was upset, that was the thing.

175

There was this report which Richard was supposed to write for his music class (a kind of music appreciation which all kids in the seventh grade take at our school, twelve weeks) and which he was in fact writing. Well, I'd seen him writing it in class and heard about it from him. Naturally he was writing about all sorts of old instruments and drawing pictures of talking Sackbuts and Serpents and Viols D'Amore and coming up to me with his sly and expectant grin and wanting to know if I knew what this and that was? But he was also writing it at home, and one evening his father took a look at Richard's report and apparently it was just the last straw for the father—there it was all scribbly and you couldn't read lots of it and there were maps and streets interspersed with accounts of Theobald Boehm inventing the flute—so the father got really angry and decided to show Richard how reports ought to be written and they sat down and talked about headings and footnotes and theses and paragraphs and documentation and clarity and so when that was all done and Richard indicated yes he understood what the issue was, the father told Richard to get going and re-write that report and he did. I felt the father understood about Richard's real ability and intelligence and knowledge and curiosity and couldn't stand it, as we all can't, that Richard wouldn't put this all to use in normal bright-kid fashion, earning normal bright-kid success and evaluation. Along with that, I could imagine the father hoping Richard would get busy and play a little ball, get in a little normal trouble for smoking in the bathroom or cutting class.

So Richard did, but in the end wasn't able to hold to it and finally produced his big music report, name up in the right-hand corner and a title and skip a space and start in with a paragraph about sackbuts and a drawing centered nicely on the page and some more writing and then *Misericordia!* sprawled across the page, as Richard's mind made some irresistible connections in Xanadu, marched a procession of talking fireplugs, of cartoon frames enclosing Duesenbergs lecturing a crowd of applauding sea horses or chesspieces about musical instruments— Oh man, give a thought to fathers at this moment!

What is a teacher's part in this whole thing? It is only to pay attention and give protection. The rest I was able to leave to Tizzo. Tizzo maintained his relationship to Richard; he insisted on remaining Richard's friend. He kept an eye out for him, instructed him on what to do or what not to do, and he played with him. They played a game in the room where Richard was a bad ill-tempered car, speeding and going through red lights and being a road hog, and Tizzo was a police car and afterwards a judge who sentenced Richard-the-car to jail and locked him up in the closet. Then he would extract promises from the bad car about being good and reforming and let him out, at which the bad car would immediately start speeding around the room and have to get arrested all over again. Richard thought he'd like to play this game every day, but Tizzo saw that was no good. He restricted Richard to one day a week, usually Friday, and only one period. Often other kids would get into the game too. Although most kids complained about Richard's childishness all week long, many of them in fact found such childishness very attractive. Since Tizzo was doing it, they could often permit themselves to play.

Tizzo, who had a father, was practicing up to be a father. He had a good use for Richard. Richard had a good use for Tizzo too, since he was learning to be a kid. Unlike the therapist and myself and Richard's own father, Tizzo didn't want Richard to turn into some other person, but only to accept the human condition. I can still hear him telling Richard forthrightly that he wasn't really a car (I know it, Tizzo, Richard would say, it's only a game) and that he could only pretend to be a car on Fridays. *That's the only day you can be a car!* Or, *Rich, I thought you were going to stop telling people to take*

177

out their dicks! Oh, yeah, Richard would say, *I was, but I forgot. Bullshit, Rich, you didn't forget,* Tizzo would say, *you just wanted to and went ahead and did it.* Sometimes Tizzo would try to explain to Richard why it was that he could call people assholes and it would be O.K., and once in a while he'd try to get Richard to call someone an asshole, just to try it out and see if he got any satisfaction out of it, but Richard didn't want to call anyone an asshole, couldn't see any reason for it, and couldn't understand what Tizzo was getting at. In the end, all Tizzo was trying to get Richard to see was that human beings had to accept the idea of being *bothered* once in a while—that was what it was about. That if you accepted that, then you also could revolt against being bothered *all* the time, and that was as free as you could be.

Occasionally Richard would get mad at the tyranny of Tizzo and produce a placard:

> Some person in the eighth grade who thinks he is tough is trying to be Julius Caesar and tell other people what to do. The whole eighth grade should get together and make him stop doing this.

Then Tizzo would get mad and say he didn't care what Richard did and if the vice-principal got him it was just tough shit and Richard would indulge himself and be a car on Monday or Tuesday. Then suddenly it would be over and I could tell when it was. The bell would ring and it would be time for Tizzo to go to Reading, which he was mad at because Eileen wouldn't let him go to the bathroom—the bell would ring and Tizzo would just stand there in the room and I'd say Get going, Tizzo, and he'd say Sorry, Mr. Herndon, I can't go to Reading, Rich just turned me into a frog! And whenever that happened, Tizzo and Richard and I and many another kid standing around would laugh like hell and I would bang Tizzo on the back as he went out and he would hit me in the ribs and Richard would skip out grinning with his arms raised up like a cheering section and we would all recognize for an instant the foolishness and absurdity of our ways through the world and feel the impact of the great, occasional and accidental joy which would be our only reward along those paths.

ABOUT THE AUTHOR

JAMES HERNDON was fired for being "unfit to teach" in the Negro ghetto school about which he wrote *The Way It Spozed to Be*. Of his experiences in this school he wrote, "I have almost no hope that there will be any significant change in the way we educate our children."

He has taught for the past ten years in a white suburb outside San Francisco, where he lives with his wife and two children.